PRAISE FOR *AWAKEN YOUR ROOTS*

"In a time of disconnection and upheaval, Lorena Saavedra Smith offers a luminous path back to wholeness—woven from the wisdom of lineage, land, and lived experience. With fierce love and grounded insight, she invites us to remember who we are, where we come from, and the power that lives in our bones."

Tara Brach, PhD
author of *Radical Acceptance* and *Trusting the Gold*

"*Awaken Your Roots* is medicine—a lovingly crafted invitation to return to our roots in the living world. Drawing on Andean wisdom, Lorena Saavedra Smith calls us to tend our wounds from generational trauma—and shows us how. Her work is a song-prayer for wholeness, a ritual of remembrance, a guide to live in right relationship with ourselves and the earth."

Valarie Kaur
bestselling author of *See No Stranger* and *Sage Warrior*
and founder of the Revolutionary Love Project

"Lorena takes you along on her journey. Navigating the hopes, dreams, and disappointments of a life spanning many cultures, she shows you how to embrace your roots and live from that place of ancient knowing as it is lived in the here and now."

Rev. Konin Cardenas, also known as Ayyā Dhammadīpā
ordained nun and Guiding Teacher of the Dassanāya Buddhist Community, author of *Gifts Greater Than the Oceans*

"Like the threads of a colorful 'manta,' *Awaken Your Roots* interweaves poetry, storytelling, philosophy, ancestral medicine, and Nature's wisdom to invite readers to reclaim agency, heal trauma, and embrace purpose in their lives. I highly recommend *Awaken Your Roots* to care providers of all backgrounds and professions as an invaluable resource for understanding the complex stories of individuals who have been 're-planted' and are searching for healing and self-acceptance in lands and cultures far away from their own."

Jennifer Kreatsoulas, PhD, C-IAYT
author of *The Courageous Path to Healing*

"These lessons in *Awaken Your Roots* have helped me understand myself and my spiritual journey. I felt in my body and soul that nature and ancestry were powerful forces in my life, but I didn't know why. Now I see why I have instinctively sought these sources of comfort and wisdom.

"As the daughter of a Latina mother who re-planted in a new land and taught me essential lessons from her personal and cultural heritage, I celebrate this book's reminder to access, trust, and lean into the spirit and guidance of our ancestral roots.

"By embracing our whole selves and our complex histories, we can carve pathways to flourishing—for ourselves and for future generations."

Kristina Graff
head of social impact with Yoga Alliance

AWAKEN YOUR ROOTS

LORENA SAAVEDRA SMITH

AWAKEN YOUR ROOTS

Reclaim Your Ancestry and Sovereignty
by Heeding the Jaguar's Call

sounds true
BOULDER, COLORADO

Sounds True
Boulder, CO

© 2025 Lorena Saavedra Smith
Foreword © 2025 Rodolfo Sánchez Garrafa

Sounds True is a trademark of Sounds True Inc.

All rights reserved. No part of this book may be used or reproduced in any manner without written permission from the author(s) and publisher.

No AI Training: Without in any way limiting the author's and publisher's exclusive rights under copyright, any use of this publication to "train" generative artificial intelligence (AI) technologies to generate text is expressly prohibited. The author reserves all rights to license uses of this work for generative AI training and development of machine learning language models.

This book is not intended as a substitute for the medical recommendations of physicians, mental health professionals, or other health-care providers. Rather, it is intended to offer information to help the reader cooperate with physicians, mental health professionals, and health-care providers in a mutual quest for optimal well-being. We advise readers to carefully review and understand the ideas presented and to seek the advice of a qualified professional before attempting to use them.

All client stories offered in this book are composites. No story reflects any specific individual, and all circumstances and names have been changed to protect identities.

Published 2025

Book design by Scribe Inc.
Cover design by Jennifer Miles
Jacket design by Rachael Murray
Illustrations © 2025 Juliet Percival
Author photo by Nelcy and Steven Baltz
Jacket photo of close-up picture of Andean textile design from Arequipa, Perú © Mark Green from Shutterstock

Printed in the United States of America

BK07141

Library of Congress Cataloging-in-Publication Data

Names: Smith, Lorena Saavedra author
Title: Awaken your roots : reclaim your ancestry and sovereignty by heeding the jaguar's call / Lorena Saavedra Smith.
Description: Boulder, CO : Sounds True, 2025.
Identifiers: LCCN 2025002603 (print) | LCCN 2025002604 (ebook) | ISBN 9781649633460 trade paperback | ISBN 9781649633477 ebook
Subjects: LCSH: Self-actualization (Psychology) | Spiritual healing | Spirituality
Classification: LCC BF637.S4 S634 2025 (print) | LCC BF637.S4 (ebook) | DDC 158.1--dc23/eng20250606
LC record available at https://lccn.loc.gov/2025002603
LC ebook record available at https://lccn.loc.gov/2025002604

Oh, beautiful little girl,
your caramel skin and black hair smells like cinnamon
and every time your bare foot kisses the ground
Earth celebrates its greatness in your perfection
Don't let the tales of the town convince you otherwise

*I am dedicating this book to you, future matriarch
and keeper of the history of your village.
My hope is for you to trust the sweetness of your heart and to
celebrate the vastness of your essence woven into Nature.*

CONTENTS

FOREWORD: MAY A THOUSAND ROOTS AWAKEN!   ix

INTRODUCTION   1

1. Reconciling with Yourself   17

2. Reconnecting with Nature   35

3. Understanding the Wound: Steps "K" and "A" of KARE: Knowing and Assessing Your Wounds   57

4. Tending the Fragmented Self: Step "R" of KARE: Reconciliation   81

5. Making the Body a Safe Place to Come Home To: Step "E" of KARE: Engendering Healing in Long-Lasting Ways   105

6. Moving Beyond Internalized Domination   127

7. Healing Through Lineage   151

8. Working with Elders and Wisdom Keepers   173

9. Embracing Your Medicine and Finding Spiritual Balance   195

CONCLUSION   219

ACKNOWLEDGMENTS   229

ABOUT THE AUTHOR   237

FOREWORD

May a Thousand Roots Awaken!

This is a book written with the wisdom of a woman who could very well be the voice of the Universal Mother. As its title expresses, it is a summons, and almost a warning, to awaken the roots that connect us to the vital force of our origin and the meaning of our existence. It is, indeed, a call that comes from telluric, volitional powers to which we must respond in order to recover our indestructible alliance with the transcendent DNA of the primordial light.

Lorena del Pilar Saavedra de Smith unfolds her reflections and proposals from the honesty of her own life. Her own experiences allow her to explore the human psyche and spirit with the utmost honesty, aware of the cultural disruptions to which we human beings are exposed in a world facing the challenges of globalization and a civilizational crisis.

It is not unusual, but rather an endemic phenomenon, that a large portion of humanity is afflicted by feelings of estrangement, uncertainty, and loss of self-control in contexts where loneliness, exclusion, and abandonment conspire against personal and collective identity, as well as against the integrity of the human being.

I see the new awakening as a reenactment of the primordial animating act of our species and its rooting in maternal soil. When we transplant a pine or alder tree, we don't expect it to stop being a pine or an alder, but rather to adapt to the environment that will host it. Similarly, when faced with different conditions, people shouldn't have to stop being who they are, but rather call into action all our capacities for biological and cultural adaptation and resilience to thrive both physically and psychologically. There is something ritualistic and enchanting about this "re-planting" that I sympathetically appreciate, given the logic it follows, the systematic way the model was developed, and above all, because of the intuitive, affective, and evocative components it rescues, as if to highlight the fabric of the lineages that will always sustain our sovereignty and restore healthy balance. Our constant concern should be not only to spread and expand freely throughout the world, but to establish ourselves with the best possible chances of success, development, and affirmation of our potential. In this way, we can all contribute to building a better world.

A woman who survived the terror prevalent in a society in turmoil and at war knows that the task of overcoming trauma confronts one with circumstances and events that make it difficult or impossible to find a reliable path to healing. Each person's emotional wounds require specific medication, appropriate and effective therapy. In many cases, refuge within a community of parishioners is merely a temporary palliative. The same is true of many healing procedures, which generate contradictions that cannot be ignored. However, the difficult harvest of experiences allows us to ascertain certain components of invaluable effectiveness, such as proving that to breathe is to live. If we breathe, it's because we are here. It's new to me to know that there are dangers in the search for reinforcements that provide stable security within the body through introspection, but it's encouraging to discover that the desired place can be found within ourselves. This is achieved by Lorena, whose encounter and confrontation with the archetypal figure of the jaguar, or *otorongo*, was the threshold to new and broad possibilities of personal affirmation.

I find that the author's account of her experiences goes far beyond the anecdotal and merely motivational, becoming the basis of an instructive methodology. It is essential for anyone interested and engaged in a similar quest to question their own situation in order to gather a scattered memory and examine the superficial layers of consciousness. It is natural for the spiritual teacher or guide to consider the cultural differences of each pilgrim. Above all, it is important to consider that, in each case, we are faced with a person whose dignity deserves all the due consideration, and this cannot be achieved through pretense.

The inner war within ourselves demands an essential reconciliation for overcoming any trauma and the subsequent reconnection with our essential selves. On this path, Lorena has achieved such reconciliation. Moreover, it is achieved through the recovery of practices of physical, mental, and spiritual union within its own traditions, which I understand to be Andean and originating from the continent fundamentally, and the results of this invaluable effort are what she now shares with us.

A primary question is: How do we connect with the exquisite architecture of nature? The answer is positioned within a philosophical framework of the Andean *Pacha* and the concept of *nuna*, conceived as a set of aspects that embody different roles. How can we make the body safe for the return of the spirit or nuna when the being has been split? This is another question addressed in close connection with the traditional worldview to which these categories belong. These and other questions are the subject of an enculturated treatment that simultaneously addresses the requirements of the aforementioned re-planting, with a notable concern for freeing the mind from all demonization that has historically affected ancestral thought. A transactional practice with the bearers of the ancient wisdom preserved by the living cultures of the Andes shapes the seriousness of this therapeutic and, in a sense, initiatory proposal. Mastery emanates from entities of power whose physical manifestations can take diverse and perhaps unsuspected forms. The idea is to be prepared to face the jaguar when it is time to answer its call. When this happens, the necessary emotional autonomy has been achieved.

The author of this book has made an important contribution to achieving a healthy balance within societies shaken by the impact of modernity, industrial revolutions, and the growing hegemony of information technology, along with the cognitive biases they give rise to.

As an anthropologist, dedicated for years to the study of symbolic structures in the Andes and to the need to make contributions to a *tinku*, or intercultural philosophical dialogue, between Western and Andean thought, I predict an auspicious path for this message, full of conviction and faith in a future without ethnic, gender, economic, or any other exclusions. *May a thousand roots awaken!*

Chorrillos-Lima, April 2025
Dr. Rodolfo Sánchez Garrafa
Quechua anthropologist
author of *Apus de los Cuatro Suyus: Construcción del Mundo en los Ciclos Mitológicos de las Deidades Montaña*
director of Markapacha
coordinator of the IntercultA Network

INTRODUCTION

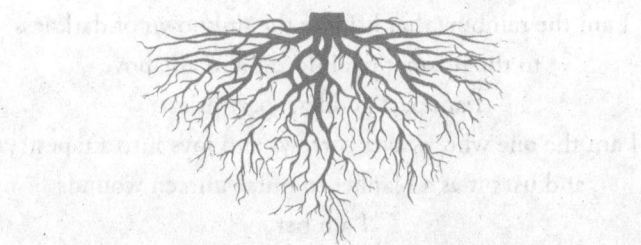

Who Am I?

I am a ray of sun with a pinch of darkness
I am the disoriented wind unleashing moods
I am the sweet waters of rivers following a path
I am the tireless ocean benefactor of life
I am the fire of a forgotten mountain
I am moist soil where the seeds rest
I am the grain that makes the crops
I am the rainbow that bridges the unknown of darkness
to the prismatic rainforest and all above
I am part goddess, part priest
I am the one who weaves sorrows and joys into a tapestry
and uses it as a blanket to nurse unseen wounds
I am her
I am a mother breastfeeding dreams
I am a sister holding pillars of sanctuaries
I am a wife rowing against the stream
I am a grandmother with overflowing secrets
I am
I am her
I am here

I started running because I sensed that I needed to do what I could to be in my body, to feel my vitality coursing through my veins. As I ran, I often had a vision of a jaguar chasing me, and I was able to connect with its energy. But a year ago, I had a powerful breakthrough. This time, I was prompted to ask myself: "Why am I running?"

In other words, *what* was I running from?

Modern psychology uses the metaphor of running from a tiger or another wild beast in its description of the fight/flight/freeze response. This metaphor sets up a relationship with Nature that turns it into the enemy. We assume that Nature is fraught with danger and obstacles—that we must do what we can to survive. Over time, this fear-based idea has led to the belief that the only way to be in relationship with Nature—with its unpredictable creatures and chaotic forces—is to outwit it . . . perhaps even by using violence or cunning. This fear-based mandate has shaped the way we relate to Nature and one another.

However, during that run, I had a beautiful epiphany. I realized that the jaguar was not chasing me so it could tear me to pieces. Instead, it was at my heels, imploring me to stop. It was saying, "Don't be afraid. I'm not here to harm you. I'm here to show you how to become one with me."

I realized that the jaguar was showing me how to face my fear with courage and determination—not by pushing through it or going around it or keeping it at a distance.

The jaguar, like the puma in the Andes, is a powerful symbol of courage and purpose across many Mesoamerican and South American cultures.

I was blessed to encounter it, for it was giving me a way to shift out of survival mode—a way of being that has proven to be harmful to our planet—and to lovingly embody liberation.

This is the principle at the core of the book you hold in your hands, *Awaken Your Roots: Reclaim Your Ancestry and Sovereignty by Heeding the Jaguar's Call*.

I wrote this book out of a desire to reclaim agency and purpose—especially from societal forces that have caused me to feel deficient, inadequate, and invisible over the years—through ancestral wisdom and a rightful relationship with Nature. The tools I've rediscovered in the ancient healing practices from my culture proved to be powerful medicine—especially for those like me: highly intuitive souls who long to deepen into their roots.

My life story includes navigating the challenges of becoming a naturalized United States citizen—but my cross-cultural journey is not my whole story. My roots are Indigenous and mixed race (*mestiza*), and I'm also a multidisciplinary Pacha philosopher. *Pacha* is a Quechua word—one of the languages of the Indigenous peoples of Perú—that encompasses everything related to Nature: time, space, and all forms of matter and energy, in all cardinal directions. Wherever you were born, and whether you identify as a migrant to the lands you find yourself in or not, we are living in a time when it's imperative for us to reconnect with who we are. Most of us have been impacted by many intersecting forms of societal sidelining, and I know that ancestral wisdom can reconnect all of us with who we truly are. It's time for us to heal, and to forge a sacred contract with Nature and all of life.

I wrote *Awaken Your Roots* for all of you who are in the tender process of rediscovering your essence and awakening to the power of sacred reciprocity, interconnectedness, and being in a living dialogue with Nature and creation. I wrote it with women like me in mind, as we are accustomed to "code-switching" for the sake of assimilating into a world that asks us to cut off entire aspects of who we are in order to survive and belong. However, anyone who has ever felt disconnected from their core essence can find solace in the words within. Throughout this book, I will use gendered terms: men, women, male, female, mother, father. I invite you to bring your own meaning to these terms, and to embrace whatever identities resonate with you.

As you read these pages, I invite you into a new, rooted belonging—one that gently asks you to reclaim everything that may have previously been a source of pain (especially the complex song of your heritage, your language, and the song of your ancestors' ways that still lives through you, though the notes may be faint). The path of reclaiming who we are and reconnecting to Nature is a long one, so this book offers ways to honor and care for yourself that go beyond the methods of today's wellness industrial complex and its well-meaning but often thoughtless appropriation of various cultural contexts.

You will be coaxed to bring into the light the parts of your personal and collective history that have been suppressed. You will be asked to sit with subjects that may be uncomfortable or painful, including trauma, infertility, violence, abuse, immigration, and the colonial legacy, and to care for yourself however you need as you face these topics with courage and sweetness. You will also discover your own medicine (which is often hiding inside your wounds, as I learned firsthand) and use it to heal yourself and be of service to the world. But first, you must be willing to find peace inside your own unhealed heart, and to acknowledge the ways that being physically and metaphorically severed from your roots has hurt you.

WE ARE MEANT TO HEAL

For so many migrants and foreign-born, the struggle to keep up while ensuring that we're a step ahead, so as to be taken seriously by the society in which we have been re-planted, can be exhausting. My mother often told me and my siblings that we had to do our best to catch up because our culture was fifty years behind Eurocentric cultures. Our ways of knowing were considered primitive and uncivilized, and we were programmed with the idea that we had to remain ahead of the curve in order to prove ourselves.

Such are the wounds of colonialism, which we are learning to unravel as we recognize that many Indigenous, non-European, and older European cultures are the holders of knowledge and wisdom connected to earth science, astronomy, medicine, healing, and other modalities that are starting to be reclaimed. Sadly, it's a slow process, as colonizing cultures stripped the civilizations they occupied of a clear sense of connection to their heritage, and we see the results of this across the world today.

Throughout the world, especially in "developed" Western countries, people spend millions of dollars on wellness products, courses, and workshops. Yet, methods for healing remain elusive to those who most need it: economically disadvantaged people and those who continue to linger on the margins of society. As this book will uncover, the implications of this are far-reaching. In a world that is beset by intergenerational trauma, an aspect of economic exploitation and historical injustice, individual healing can take us far—but until it is connected to the collective goal of overall wellness for all the beings of the world, it will only ever be for the fortunate few, while the rest stay in survival mode.

To that end, I also intend for *Awaken Your Roots* to serve as a wake-up call to researchers and practitioners whose work revolves around the power of ancestral medicine as a tool for wellness. While many of the current voices in the field are well-meaning, it's important for us to turn a more critical eye to the ways in which entitlement and assumption continue to deplete our so-called wisdom traditions. By burying the voices of the men, women, and two-spirits who have been the wisdom keepers of so many traditions that were nearly decimated and who continue to bear the wounds of these forces today, many in the wellness and spirituality world perpetuate an unacknowledged spiritual colonialism.

I hope for this book to offer a healing remedy, and to give guidance onto a different path. And to those of you who have often felt you didn't belong, I hope to resuscitate the voices of all our ancestors who were silenced. This book will be a compassionate guide that will provide ways to soothe the emotional distress that is the result of the wounds of surviving in a world that was not meant for our thriving. As *Awaken Your Roots* shares, we are the ones we've been waiting for, and our ancestors live in and through us. When we access their wisdom, we discover what we need to flourish and to create a world that is deserving of us.

THE INFLUENCE OF SACRED RECIPROCITY

Thankfully, there is a way out of surviving and into flourishing. The wisdom we hold is wisdom we carry in our bones, in the songs of our mother tongue, in the vibrant dirt of our birthlands, in the delicious foods our ancestors cooked, in our cleansing tears, in our bodies—which are vessels for the knowledge and traditions our ancestors lovingly passed on through the millennia. Although this knowledge is not often valued by mainstream society, it is the most important knowledge we can cultivate. It is time-honored, empirical, and rooted in our lived experiences and our very DNA.

Many of us are awakening to the potency of the ways and wisdom of our ancestors. Many of us are awakening to the beauty of our cultural traditions. At the same time, we cannot make the mistake of romanticizing ancestral work; reconciliation with our roots can only happen because something got broken! This means that ancestral work can be *painful*—whether the people in our lineages were victims or perpetrators. Often, for many of us, it's a combination of both. We must approach healing with care and compassion. Sometimes, we may not be ready to put the pieces of our family tree back together, and that's okay.

Please know that this book won't go into elaborate or prescribed rituals and ceremonies, as I am not interested in appropriating aspects of my culture. Here's the good news, though: nourishment is close at hand. The vast majority of Indigenous cultures have one root base, and that's Nature. In Andean philosophy and religion, connecting with Nature from a nonextractive, nonexploitative perspective—with reciprocity and respect—allows us to be in the right relationship with the Earth and with ourselves. Nature is the grandmother who records the history of our pain and our triumph, so we can always connect with it when we need to heal our wounds and when we require more strength to embrace our roots.

This is how the Andean people sustained a vibrant and thriving culture—through something known in the Quechua language as *Sumaq*

Kawsay, or "living well." Living well is a fundamental holistic philosophy that promotes maintaining balance and harmony with Nature in order to flourish. It encompasses the Andean people's approach to social and communal life, economics, education, agriculture, science, the arts, and spirituality. This approach to collective well-being is often at odds with the individualistic mindset many of us in Western culture have become accustomed to—a mindset that promotes profit, commodification, growth over stability, and individual health over communal health. When we explore what it means to live well, we can find freedom and release from the phantoms of our wounding and finally do the work of creating the world we deserve.

If you've chosen to read this book now, it's because you've been called. You know that you no longer have to endure your own self-destruction—which impacts every single one of us in the way it wrenches us from a supportive relationship with Nature. You don't have to travel a thousand miles, using fuel to arrive at a place where someone will give you a magical elixir that will make you feel whole and restored. Healing can be found in your own backyard, in a restorative connection with Nature.

Reconnecting with Nature is the key to reconnecting with our roots and ancestry, overcoming adversity, and committing to healing the wounds of history. This will also enable us to step into more loving, respectful relationships with individuals and societies very different from us, without falling into the trap of othering, comparison, and conquest.

WEAVING A NEW AND ANCIENT WAY OF BEING

I'm an integrated therapist who has assisted hundreds of women in healing from challenging situations ranging from poverty, to abuse, to war, to an outright dismissal of who they really are by society at large. I have extended my heartfelt support to all of them, because I know what it's like to experience self-erasure and to be unseen and unheard by others. Over the years, I discovered multiple disciplines that support the integration of wholeness—uniting our body, emotions, and thinking mind. All of these practices have been useful, but only to a point.

It was when I took a leap of faith and dove deep into the knowledge and companionship of Nature that I remembered the multidimensional, intergenerational knowledge that lives in my bones. It was through Nature that I became whole—by applying the ancestral medicine that was already in my DNA.

What I offer you in *Awaken Your Roots* is a path of courage, radical intimacy, and unapologetic truth. I provide multidisciplinary solutions and suggestions for finding your path to reconnect with the medicine you've always carried within you, but which has remained dormant and asleep under the spell of fear, trauma, grief, and pain. My wish is for you to be who you really are, so that you can embrace your gifts and unleash your medicine to heal yourself, your family, and your community. I will walk with you and let Nature and your ancestors guide me to be the best mirror and reflection I can be. As you walk this path, you not only reconcile with your roots and therefore heal yourself, you also contribute to the healing of all those who came before and all those who will come after you.

Throughout this book, the sleek and elegant jaguar will be our guide. The jaguar allows us to embody the sensate experience of being alive on this planet. Throughout what is now called Mesoamerica and South America, big cats like the jaguar and the puma represent power; in Pacha philosophy, they are the protectors of humanity as we walk in this realm of existence. In many ancestral traditions, when they arrive, it's a powerful sign of transformation. The one who encounters them is said not to be a regular human being but someone who has the potential to change the trajectory of their life. This is why I was so humbled when the jaguar showed up in my vision. Although I didn't know it then, it was initiating me into a vital aspect of my own life's work.

The medicine of this book is meant to attune you to this immense liberatory energy, so you can weave a new reality that is grounded in an ancient wisdom that will reverberate across past, present, and future. The concept of weaving is dear to me and to many Indigenous cultures. Rather than "building" or "constructing" a reality vertically, from the ground up, we weave horizontally in a collaborative relationship with one another and the planet. We literally weave ourselves into what the late Vietnamese Buddhist teacher Thich Nhat Hanh referred to as "interbeing," which creates deep personal and collective healing.

As a practitioner of Pacha philosophy, it is my honor to weave the knowledge I offer in *Awaken Your Roots* in relationship with my own ancestors and with Nature. Where I come from, the women weave beautiful *mantas*, or shawls, with each thread representing everyone who came before us and everyone who will come after us. The act of weaving is also evident in the braids that the women of the Andean region wear.

My desire is that this book will be a metaphorical manta you feel cocooned within, as well as a braid that you are lovingly woven into. Rather than feeling that you're carrying the weight of the world on your shoulders, the embrace of this manta will help you recognize that you're never alone—you're woven into the fabric of our interconnectedness. You're supported by a deep wisdom that will serve to make you feel centered, such that you won't feel disconnected from your roots or made to feel "less than."

ABOUT THIS BOOK

The first two chapters of this book are foundational in our journey, because they are about reconnecting with ourselves and with Nature, both of which are essential when it comes to soothing our hearts and nervous systems. We have to know our story and where we come from, and remember that Nature is the essential ground of our being, before we can move into greater levels of individual and collective healing. This is where I also introduce the elements of Nature—water, wind, fire, and earth—which are instrumental in Pacha philosophy and many Indigenous traditions around the world. Through the elements, we'll come to understand and make peace with our own personal story, and to reestablish a connection with Nature. If you have no familiarity with your ancestry, the elements will be the tools to which we will continually return and that can guide you through the process of reconciliation with your lineage.

Spiritual bypassing can run rampant in the "wellness" world, but in order to understand how we got here, we must come to a deeper understanding of our wounds. Chapter 3 helps us to do this. I also share a method we'll continually revisit throughout the book, which I refer to by the acronym KARE:

- *Knowing* and identifying the wound, and recognizing that something happened, which translates to seeing the jaguar (discussed in chapter 3).

- *Assessing* the dimensions of the breakage (of the heart, of harmony, of balance, etc.), which helps us get clear about the "why" behind the trauma, as well as its impact on our life, which in turn allows us to evaluate our relationship with the jaguar (discussed in chapter 3).

- *Reconciling* what is out of order and calling our *nuna*, or what the Western world refers to as "the soul," back to integrate with the self. This can be likened to meeting the jaguar (discussed in chapter 4).

- *Engendering* ongoing remedies to breed our own healing, well-being, and reconciliation with our nuna—which is akin to embodying the jaguar's coat and legs (discussed in chapter 5).

The KARE method is a process that calls us into a place of compassionate self-witnessing and deep presence. It will also ask us to dance between tightening, softening, and releasing—similar to how the human heart works.

In chapter 4, using Pacha philosophy, I define nuna as containing a number of different aspects that embody different roles; this includes the part of a person's essence that can leave the physical body when trauma occurs. It is important to recognize that nuna and the body are inextricable; although they can sometimes appear separate, they are not unrelated. The work you'll be doing throughout this book is all about

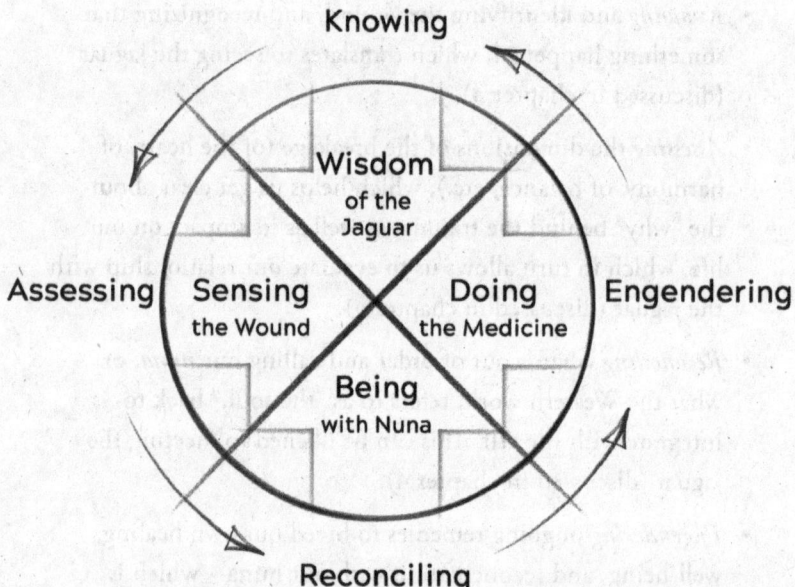

KARE → original method by Lorena Saavedra Smith
- Knowing
- Assessing
- Reconciling
- Engendering

A multidirectional and embodied method for restoring *munay* (the feeling, loving, and willpower heart) through compassionate self-witnessing. This practice invites you to explore the roots of your wounds, patch fragmented parts of your manta, and realign with the elements. It's a sacred process of healing with deep presence and reverence.

making the body, mind, and external environment (including land and home) a safe place to come back to. Overall, in healing yourself, it is your responsibility to bring your nuna closer by nurturing your body and your relationship with the world.

Chapter 5 delves into the importance of making the body safe to come back into. In many ways, the process of coming back to ourselves and restoring balance among all the pieces of ourselves can make us hypervigilant, as if we have to relinquish everything about our past in order to heal, including anything that might be viewed as oppressive, such as the spiritual tradition we grew up in. However, building self-trust goes a lot deeper than adhering to external definitions of what we should and should not honor. It's also about recognizing and learning to work with your intuition and learning to take back your autonomy from the places where you may have left it.

Chapter 6 picks up where chapter 5 left off. Learning to trust ourselves and develop a strong relationship with the body as well as the environment in which we live, either where our seed was planted (our birthland) or re-planted (in the land we have come to inhabit), is important. But I've found that even when we are successful at this, we might still feel ill at ease or inferior, due to the internalization of domination and other forms of abuse. This is why individual healing will never be enough. To that end, I present potential solutions and methods of inquiry to help us really understand the impact of cultural insensitivity and cultural wounding on our individual experiences of living in a world that privileges certain people over others.

Chapter 7 covers the power of healing by weaving our own remedies for pain and trauma, based on our connection with our ancestors. Although it can be inspiring to work with different traditions, it is deeply therapeutic to reconcile with the traditions of our own ancestors. I share a little of my own story of healing my interpretation of religion. As someone with roots in both the Catholic Church and Indigenous traditions, I know the importance of not demonizing the spirituality we may have grown up within. Instead, we can do the work of separating the ways humans have used religion to dominate others from the sacred aspects of religion. This can expand our methods of healing as we come into a more authentic relationship with our background.

Chapter 8 goes into the value of working with trusted teachers and elders. For many people on a path of reconciliation, expansion occurs when we have a wise and compassionate mirror who accurately reflects us back to ourselves. The experience of teaching and the stewardship of ancient traditions is one that exists in a much more transactional way in our modern world, which is why it's important to be discerning on the path of working with a trusted teacher. It's also important to recognize that a teacher can come in many different forms—it might not be a beloved relative or older person, but a tree or a mountain!

The final chapter covers a range of inquiries. First, we investigate what it means to locate, find, and manifest our specific medicine for the world. If we have a crisis in confidence, we must resource ourselves by tapping into the elements of Nature and recognizing that our sovereignty is our birthright. I'll guide you into a renewed understanding of purpose, viewed through the lens of our elemental connections. With a sense of ritual, you can let go of that which creates imbalance and disrupts harmony, and rely on Pacha to help reestablish order. In this way, you can meet the jaguar head-on and live from that place, which will help you share your gifts in a more vibrant and intentional manner. We'll discuss the ethics of doing this so that we aren't operating from an aspect of ourselves that's disconnected from the manta of life, but from a sense of agency that is committed to supporting others—even perceived "enemies"—and our true abundance.

At the beginning of each chapter, you'll find a poem I've written that encapsulates the themes within; because poetry involves metaphors, I welcome your interpretation, which will impact the way you receive the teachings. For me, poetry is a form of understanding that transcends the thinking mind and offers texture to our experiences and inner knowing. I am including poetry for those like myself, who derive meaning not just from words but from the sacred meaning behind them.

MIRROR AND EMBODY THE JAGUAR

The exercise sections in each chapter are in two forms: Mirror the Jaguar, where you'll be guided through active self-inquiry, and Embody the Jaguar, where you'll engage in activities that will be informed by your explorations and some of the themes of Pacha philosophy that you'll find within each chapter. These exercises are meant to bring you into a state of active pause, balance, and harmony. I suggest you read the chapters and do the exercises in order, as the themes of each chapter build on the last; altogether, they give you an integrated experience of facing the jaguar.

While the exercises include self-inquiry questions, you don't have to journal on each question. Writing has been a marvelous tool for us human beings, but in many parts of the world, it is not the primary method of self-expression. I ask that you attune to the most primal aspect of who you are, or the part of you that's capable of connecting with the jaguar, as you undertake the inquiries. You may choose to dance, stomp your feet, make sounds, sing songs, create sculptures, weave, etc. When you make contact with the jaguar like this, it should not be through the construct of your mind; you are not trying to "understand" or to interpret your experience, but to express it—and sometimes this will be in ways the rational mind will not necessarily understand. I encourage you to lean back and "be" the elements themselves.

You will notice that many of the chapters focus on unpacking and understanding the root causes of our personal and collective wounds—which is extremely important in the process of healing our wounded hearts and waking up from the dis-order of the splintered modern world, which has made many of us feel so separate from Nature. However, this is not a book about trauma, per se. There are many wonderful resources about trauma written by everyone from mental health experts to therapists and medical doctors. I am less interested in using these frameworks, most of which fall under a Western scientific model, and more interested in bringing us back to a holistic awareness of dis-order and what we can do about it. Many of our ancestors held this sacred knowledge, and it still lives inside us, waiting to be uncovered so that we can return to our innate Nature.

This book is, at its heart, a book about emotional autonomy. But in order to cultivate emotional autonomy, you will want to ensure that you can call upon a number of different resources, some of which will not be purely mental or emotional. The work of embodying the jaguar is ferocious but it's also vulnerable—for the jaguar experiences both courage and fear. As you work with principles, such as the KARE method, please ensure that you are adequately supported to experience the full spectrum of your primal Nature.

Awaken Your Roots is a direct and loving voice that is also corrective—not for the purpose of "fixing" you, but more like a grandmother who will tell you exactly how you may be holding yourself back, while giving you the support to find a way forward. It carries a message that I hope will be valuable for all of us: It is possible to reconcile with our true self—the self that is never broken, because all of us are a part of Nature.

As one thread of the manta, I hope to guide you to re-member—literally to put back together—who you truly are: the expert of your own life, the one who has the grace and strength to heal, the one who has the strength to restore that which you may have believed was lost. And in the process, may you roar with the power, love, confidence, and multidimensional, awe-inspiring wisdom of the jaguar!

1
RECONCILING WITH YOURSELF

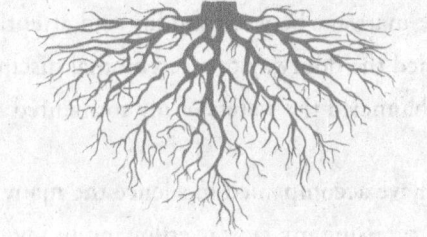

I Touch Earth in Gratitude

Because of you, I found the path back to my body.
I learned that my strength is capable of molding, expanding, contracting,
and taking the forms of other species beyond my human complexity.

Through presence and guidance to welcome my breath as a loyal ally,
I discovered places within me that were covered with clay and shame,
and the sweetness of your melodies offered me a needed shelter to
rest and restore, so I could keep going.

The marriage between fluidity and attention
opened the doorway to a ceremonial discipline
that channeled the waters of my tormented rivers.

In disbelief, I have accompanied in silence the many roads of tears
caressing my face, overflowing in joy,
and I have witnessed the power of being in my body
beyond the anticipation of the future and the regrets of the past.

You, my beloved yoga and meditation practices,
became so intimate to me,
I now make love to myself a ritual.

You believed in me and stood up for me on stormy days,
assuring me that I am connected to something bigger
than what my human eyes can see.

You showed me the path back to my human body and
that living and breathing in my brown skin,
covering my ancient blood,
is sacred, legitimate, and pure.

And today, as I hear the voice of my sister the crow chatting,
and my breath recognizes the sweetest of my winds,
and my waters mixed with salt follow the course of contentment,
standing like a mountain
I humbly kneel to earth celebrating that I came home safe.

You gave me the keys to my freedom,
and from the other side of the threshold,
where I am embracing the healing connection with my lands,
I say thank you for what you have done.

I want to take this moment to formally introduce myself to you. My name is Lorena del Pilar Saavedra de Smith, which combines my Peruvian family's roots and my US husband's family name. I had the choice to change my name when I became a US citizen, and I did. I shortened my name to Lorena Smith, as I knew that having a more Anglicized surname would make my life easier. However, I kept a piece of my identity by making Saavedra my middle name.

Many foreign-born carry a complex relationship with their culture. I am no different. Pride in the tongue and traditions of one's lineage is often mixed with a sense of loss, grief, and the specific circumstances that may have led them to leave their country of origin. Often, in moving to a new place where the dominant culture is a world apart from the one in which you grew up, you are faced with two primary options that can leave you feeling torn and incomplete: assimilate and lose your language and traditions, or don't assimilate and face the shame of being perceived as different or "less than." Assimilation is a domestication of the primal self into the larger culture, for the sake of survival. Many of us learn to live with the paradox by dancing between these choices, constantly negotiating between two seemingly separate selves but never quite able to bring them together.

Of course, there's also another option: some call it *acculturation*—which leaves the choice to us as to how we might integrate our original cultural identity with our new cultural environment. We are learning that it's not either/or, especially as we go through our reconciliation process, which allows us to weave together all aspects of who we are to exist in a delicate balance. A term I prefer to acculturation is *re-planting*. When we re-plant ourselves in a new land and new circumstances, we consciously adopt things from our new culture, retain aspects of our original culture, and leave out that which we have decided no longer serves us. We re-plant ourselves in new soil. And like any plant that is removed from its original habitat and rooted into a new land, we will grow in a way that is unique to our own temperament, history, and potential.

But of course, these are not simple, clear-cut, individual choices that we can recognize early in our path. They are usually accompanied by a larger reality: one of intergenerational trauma, and loss of our connection to Nature and all of life. My story is a testament to this.

Growing up in a congested, multiethnic, colorful, and violent Lima in the 1980s amid civil war wasn't easy. I learned from a very young age to be aware of danger and always be prepared for a catastrophe. Children in other parts of the world might have spent their early years in relative comfort, focused on school and play. But like a lot of children in the so-called developing world, I learned from an early age to run and hide from the sound of bombs or predators lying in wait in the shadows to pounce on vulnerable young girls. Like too many children in parts of the world that are torn apart by violence and domination, I was a survivor of terror.

The reality is, we cannot deny that thousands of people who migrate to foreign lands bring with them similar stories, and it cannot be denied that there are plenty of people who grow up with lack of access to things like water, housing, health care, and education in the US and across the world. There are limited resources to address their unique emotional needs—which is why I have decided to write this book. I know that although some people might argue that it's cowardice that leads people to leave their countries of origin to find a "better life," it's important to consider the various reasons anyone chooses to leave—reasons that range from escaping financial hardship to getting away from state-sanctioned violence, etc.

These issues do not happen in a vacuum. It's easy to point fingers and assign blame, but we are all interconnected. In order to heal, we must recognize the ways in which our connectedness can both cause harm (e.g., colonialism, coercive influence, and other forms of domination) and be a balm for healing (e.g., healthy and respectful cultural exchange). I know from my own story and the stories of so many people I've met that it takes great courage and strength to journey to a foreign land where sometimes the language and lifestyle are totally different from anything we've ever known, and to leave behind people and places we love in order to make a new life for ourselves and our family.

However, the quest for a better life does not come without a high cost. Eventually, I would come to see that my emotional wounds were actually an initiation into my specific medicine. Over the years, through my own healing processes, I cultivated the ability to welcome my strength, which supported the healing of my heart and my mind. But first, I had to live through a lot of strife in my process of adapting to my "new normal" in the land that granted me an opportunity for which I am grateful. Like many, I am no stranger to the confusing immigration system, a web in which many get caught for extended periods. Like many, aside from being homesick, I faced the deteriorating impacts of stress and anxiety due to language barriers, financial struggles, and disconnection from my family of origin. Because I came to the US on a student visa, I was tasked with becoming my own caregiver and provider, all while navigating a system I was not familiar with. Suddenly, I didn't have several generations of family members to care for me. In the land that prioritizes individualism, it was all on me as to whether I had enough money to pay for school, eat, put a roof over my head, and look out for my physical and mental health. The levels of anxiety were at times so unmanageable that I needed medication to combat my self-destructive thoughts and actions.

I know I am not alone—and today, right now, I bow to the strength of those who have committed no crimes yet face the uncertainty of immigration policies and the fear of criminalization and deportation.

While the medication for my mental health worked to help maintain my sanity, and my trips to the local Latino church for Sunday services made me feel like I was held by a loving community, the comfort I experienced didn't last very long. In moments of clarity, I had conversations with my inner critic, who was the epitome of self-judgment. Every single one of us struggles with the voice of the inner critic, but when this voice is compounded by racial and xenophobic bias, and the general sense of being invisible and unheard in a society that does not value you, you might start to believe it.

At times, I felt like a puzzle piece that didn't quite fit. I knew there was something missing. I kept falling to my knees, asking the God of my understanding to have mercy on me and take away this horrible emptiness that was killing me from the inside out. Like so many re-planted people who journey to new lands for opportunities, I wasn't here to do harm or take advantage of my new chance at life; I was here to study, work hard, serve in the community, and thrive.

At first, I found my way home to myself through yoga and meditation because it was more affordable than therapy, which gave me a sense of relief from the inner critic and a foundation for establishing peace and balance. However, I was once again caught in a conflict. It took me many months to confess to my highly Catholic family that I was doing something that went against their belief systems, as yoga and meditation weren't part of the tradition I was raised in. Many re-planted women face this contradiction in the process of healing. Often, they are torn between liberating themselves from the more restrictive tenets of their home culture, but they want very much to feel a sense of connection to their roots.

As a young person, I had been trained to follow the rules. Even though yoga and meditation were helping me, I was concerned and afraid that I would burn in hell for eternity for daring to explore different pathways to freedom. As painful as it was, I continued in my quest to find peace and freedom in my new country. I was open to whatever came my way.

I still remember the day I decided to stop in at a local yoga studio to take a "free first class." These types of healing modalities were way out of my price range, and I could not afford them. For months, I pounced on all the opportunities available to take a free first class (sometimes, a free first month) at every wellness center within a fifteen-mile radius of where I lived. This adventure of going from center to center also gave me the chance to sample all the different and available methods and "lineages" of these ancient technologies. Some of the methods were more movement- and body-based, some of them were focused on the mastery of the energy that resides within us, some had a more spiritual basis, and others used their own peculiar blend of ideas to adjust the ancient teachings to their own agendas—which were often dictated by the desire for money, power, and fame. However, one of the things that remained consistent across these different approaches was a sense of fidelity to the breath. All these different forms aimed for the union between the conscious and unconscious mind, between the body and the soul. The breath was a vehicle toward liberation. Discovering my breath, what I call my wind, gave me the opportunity to live again. Every time I practiced conscious breathing was a reminder of new cycles, new life, rebirth. I understood that if I was breathing, I was here.

Of course, back in those days, the practice was not as mainstream as it is now. My mind and body were opening to a new way of being, but I still had to contend with the elitism of navigating spirituality in an environment that saw me as "the other," and sometimes as the cleaning lady. Being a practitioner who lived in financial distress and existed in a brown body that spoke English with a thick accent had clear disadvantages. However, my inner fortitude kept bringing me back. Even though I sometimes felt that I didn't fit in, I continued to focus on the positive changes I experienced with respect to my body and my growing self-compassion, not to mention the way I was learning to meet the world—with a firm handshake, confident eye contact, and the growing awareness that I mattered.

A while after I exhausted all my chances to sample what was out there, I committed to one yoga studio, where their classes and teachings offered me a sense of stability. I was given new tools to feel my body and all the emotions trapped within. This was also new for me, because I was always so used to running away from my emotions, and I was conditioned to never look inside. Instead, I had been trained to look "up" and ask God for mercy—and to keep moving forward. I realized that these habits functioned as coping tools—things I had learned from my family and wounds that had been passed down by my ancestors who did whatever they could to stay alive. However, this is not healthy conditioning. It reinforces the idea that we are unsafe inside our own body, and that it's dangerous to search for the roots of our thoughts, emotions, and physical ailments through introspection.

In the next few years, I would come to make peace with the part of myself that was constantly encouraging me to keep moving forward because it was operating from self-preservation. But at this early point in my journey, I needed to seek a different path. As much as I missed home, I realized that the home I was looking for was inside myself, a place where I'd always felt discomfort and mistrust, not to mention abuse. I was also looking for freedom from the painful memories that were buried inside me. I was looking for freedom from the shame and the belief that I was no better than a sewer rat, forced to hide in the shadows. I was looking for freedom from my own and other people's judgments of how I looked and sounded, especially when I was attempting to express myself in a language that was not my first language. I was looking for freedom from my poverty mentality, which had kept me from boldly asking to be paid the right amount of money for my hard work—all out of the fear of losing my job, which some part of me didn't even believe I deserved. I was looking for freedom from the toxic and abusive relationships that had stolen the last ounces of self-love I had and continued to put me in violent situations, which reinforced my distrust in others. I was looking for freedom from the mindset of victimhood, which made me believe everyone was against me, and that I needed to be ready to defend myself, even against those who showed sincere interest in my well-being.

I was looking for freedom to be myself. I was ready to stop running away from the jaguar, and I chose to stop in order to face it, surrender to its care, and be one with it. I wanted to embody my wounds with pride and humbly stand up and be the jaguar to others.

MIRROR THE JAGUAR
Primal Journaling

- As you read my story, were there parts of it that you could identify with? How did you feel in your own body as I shared my own account of trauma? What did this activate inside you?

- Take ten to fifteen minutes to journal your own life story. Be primal with this. Feel free to write backwards and forwards—language may not even be needed. You may wish to draw symbols, use lines and dots, etc. Remember, language is a construct of the thinking mind, and you are being encouraged to filter from the gut to the heart to the mind to your hands. This is the way of the jaguar. Write about your own experiences of suffering and trauma, as well as your path of healing. Once you're done with this process, don't look at what you came up with. Instead, do something to ground your body, like taking a nap, taking time to go out into Nature and put your feet or hands in the dirt, or whatever feels right for you.

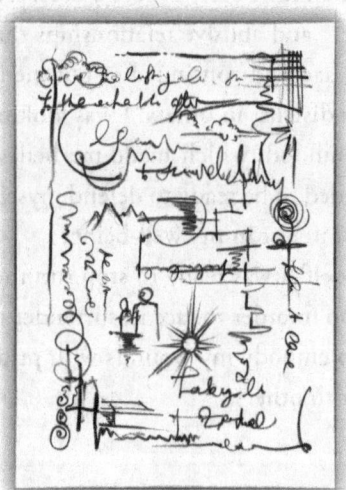 

Primal journaling invites us to tell our life story in raw, symbolic form. With intuitive lines, spirals, dots, and other forms, it becomes a personal language of expression— bridging emotions from the gut, heart, and mind to the page.

- Take some time before you come back to what you wrote, drew, or expressed. Without judging or evaluating any of it, consider how these experiences intertwine with the collective story of suffering, trauma, and healing. What are the larger themes (intergenerational trauma, mental illness, colonialism, gendered violence, etc.) that are a part of your story?

- Write down any lingering questions about your path, as well as any deep desires you have for your path of re-membering (literally bringing together all parts of the whole) and discovery (literally removing the cover with intention to see what is underneath).

MY PATH TOWARD SPIRITUAL RECONCILIATION

Throughout my early healing journey, I began to notice some of the ways the spiritual teachings I was discovering at the time had been dangerously refashioned into a one-size-fits-all mindset that didn't take into account differences in cultural background and the unique paths that every single one of us must take toward our own path and calling. Although the ancient technologies of mindfulness and yoga helped me to identify the things that were keeping me from feeling safe, happy, and whole, I came across a lot of unskilled methods of teaching that put a huge dent in my process of recovering from trauma—both childhood trauma and the trauma of navigating a new environment without the proper resources to support me. I noticed the ways in which the teachers I met avoided discussions around intersectionality—which is something that helps us understand how our specific experiences around things like race/ethnicity, class, gender, sexual orientation, ability, and identity shape our walk through the world. Not many were talking about the way that our access or lack of access can make it easier or harder for some of us to acquire the resources we need.

I have my own version of this experience. One night, I ended up at a fancy wellness center. I was emotionally and mentally in a state of imbalance and disharmony, but I was also determined to care for myself. I had a blue yoga mat from Salvation Army, shoes from Target, and secondhand clothes from a thrift store. I still recall placing my shoes in the little cabinet and noticing all the expensive items the other students had left behind. I definitely felt out of my element! To make matters worse, the woman at the front desk looked me up and down and blurted out, "Are you here to clean the studio?" My heart sank but I firmly said, "No. And here's my fifteen dollars to pay for tonight's class."

As I lay in a resting pose, the teacher applied an essential oil to my forehead. In that moment, I knew that I would one day have a wellness center and that I would one day talk about all of this. I would talk about how disconnected the woman at the front desk had been—about how this class was my only medicine, and she had almost taken it from me. I would talk about my recognition that people can be oblivious to others' humanity and wholeness—and that too often, we are taught to see a label rather than a person when we encounter the world around us. I knew that if I continued to do the work, I'd someday open the door to welcome everyone, especially those whose experiences resonate with mine, and I'd offer a sanctuary where we all could rest. I did exactly this, many years later, when I opened a wellness center in Tampa, Florida. I welcomed everyone from women wearing burqas to people praying with rosaries, as I burned palo santo and sprayed agua florida to anoint the space.

However, the deeper I got into the yoga world, the more things continued to shift for me. I kept noticing that even in places that preached inclusivity, there was a highly entitled approach to working with these technologies, and a general lack of cultural sensitivity. I saw people wearing bindis and other sacred symbols, or using images of Hindu deities for decoration, because they were considered cool or fashionable. I encountered others using Sanskrit and chanting mantras without knowing their deeper meaning—instead relying on questionable English translations with little to no investigation or sense of connection to the originating spirituality and culture. In fact, more and more of the dominant "gurus" I encountered were of European descent. Luckily, I had some Hindu friends and coworkers who were kind enough to let me into their inner circle, which is when I saw firsthand that cultural appropriation was a huge monster I didn't want to be a part of.

In addition, it seemed like the most "valuable" perspective toward mindfulness was couched in a modern, scientific approach. It seemed that everywhere I went, people were talking about evidence-based metrics. I realized this was because the Western mindset is one that seeks to understand things by measuring them. There is nothing wrong with this approach in and of itself, but it can also take the aliveness and spirit out of a sacred practice. Also, unsurprisingly, this metrics-based mindset has been used to "optimize" things like "performance" and "engagement." In other words, mindfulness has become commodified to yield a profit.

I yearned for transparency and a deeper inquiry into how we could benefit from these impactful teachings without losing sight of the ways that cultural theft (through colonialism and commodification) can create conflict. We must look at how these teachings are being interpreted and by whom. Moreover, whom are they actually meant to serve?

Of course, I didn't have the language for my concerns, which felt hard to voice, much less understand. However, I noticed that there were times when I walked away from classes feeling drained. Drained by hiding my ethnic identity and choosing to be "less Latina" in an attempt to fit in. Drained by choosing not to listen to the still, small voice within that told me, *This teaching seems incomplete. They're talking about dissolving separation, returning to wholeness, and the union of mind and body, self and higher consciousness. Sure, that might be true on a fundamental level, but it doesn't address the fact that not all of us feel safe enough to live in our bodies.*

At some point, though, I realized that I could choose to retain the positive aspects. Yoga and mindfulness meditation had given me ways to make peace with my mind and body, and I was grateful for that. But I had deeper work to do. It was time for a reconciliation process.

Reconciliation is defined as "the restoration of friendly relations." As I have come to discover on my path, most of us have a war raging within. We are at war with ourselves—with the parts of us that we've abandoned or terrorized, or that have been abandoned and terrorized by the culture at large. Reconciliation brings us into greater intimacy with ourselves. Instead of continuing to churn in the—understandably valid—raging conflict between native soil and new environment, assimilation and marginalization, right and wrong, tradition and modernity, all of which teaches us to run away from the jaguar, we learn to come back to ourselves in the spirit of compassion and nonjudgment—noticing the places where we have felt confused and uprooted, the places where we need to compost our pain, and the places where we long for revitalization and connection to our deepest self. Reconciliation is also about reconnecting to our roots in such a way that we can stand tall and be proud of who we are; we can let our voice be heard, whether it sounds like a quiet stream or a roaring tempest. For me, reconciliation came from considering where I came from—my spiritual DNA that helped me to orient myself and experience my wholeness.

Like most women who grew up in a spiritual or religious household and who were later re-planted from their ancestral lands in new places like the United States, I learned to pray and stay connected to the God of my understanding, which helped me get through my trials and tribulations. I spent most of my childhood and youth involved in church activities along with cleansing, purification, and ritualistic ceremonies. My mind and heart overflowed with beautiful memories filled with prayers for healing, rosary beads, agua florida, candles, palo santo, incense, coca leaves, and many earthly representations of the divinity that hail from my Andean heritage, since I come from a very syncretic culture where Catholicism and Indigenous traditions are woven together. These items came in different colors and shapes. I experienced the holiness of everything associated with Nature: holy water, holy fire, holy movements and gestures, holy silence—the list is endless.

Little did I know that this way of embracing spirituality—as a manta, a Latin American term for a shawl woven of components that all connect back to Nature—would eventually help me to reconcile with my roots, heal my disconnection, and mold my career as a successful therapist who advocates for the integration of ancestral knowledge that supports reconciliation with self and others. In truth, my spiritual roots gave shape to my life and helped me put the pieces back together when there were no coaches, mentors, mental health professionals, or bodies of conventionally accepted knowledge that could offer me sustained support.

Of course, people might say, "Well, Lorena, you used yoga to get you through a rough time, didn't you? That wasn't part of your roots."

To which I say, "Yes!" I am so grateful to yoga, and to the ancient wisdom behind this sacred practice. Yoga was like an antibiotic that stopped the infection and aided my body's healing and balance. At a certain point, though, I had to ask myself the important question: Would I continue to overharvest this medicine by commodifying it and taking it further from its roots, or would I use the discipline it had given me to find a way to become centered within my own roots? I didn't want to continue to exploit and overharvest this medicine that had brought me back to balance. What I wanted was to use the strength it had given me to go through my own reconciliation process and recover practices of physical, mental, and spiritual union within my own traditions.

These days, I have so much respect for yoga that I don't practice as much as I used to. Let me explain what I mean by that. Yoga, especially the external practices, sparked and activated my discovery of the embodied practices of my own culture. I sense that there is a portion of me that is drawn to yoga, perhaps because my "seed" received winds blown in from India and South Asia, but I also understand that the purpose of this lifetime is to recuperate and practice the traditions of my own lineage. For example, Andean philosophy includes a great deal of embodiment practices, including dancing and celebratory movements to connect with the Sun and awaken Earth, to connect with the elements, and to salute the four directions and three worlds. These days, the "asanas" of my yoga practice have matured into primal movements that make sense to my body and spiritual DNA.

Yoga gave me back my body, and mindfulness meditation gave me back my mind, but maybe we can view phenomena like yoga through a more nuanced lens. Accessibility to a wide variety of bodies, with different abilities and from different socioeconomic and racial/ethnic strata, is very important. But how do we celebrate the evolutionary gifts of yoga without diluting its original wisdom? In making a healing modality more accessible, is it possible to retain the sacred properties that brought it into existence? Is it possible to bring forth a world in which healing modalities are not just accessible to a range of bodies, but also honor the people who hail from the culture and tradition that planted and nurtured the seeds of the practice? Beloved reader, please pause to ask yourself these questions. You may never have previously considered them, but the healing journey asks us to exercise a new awareness, which may cause us to question what we may have taken for granted.

Overall, your healing journey is a path home to yourself. If there's anything I want you to take away from my story, it's that no matter how downtrodden or on the outskirts of society you've felt, reconciliation with your true self, your roots and authentic grace and radiant soul, is possible.

Claiming our story without the need to hide or gloss over the more painful parts is what makes us stronger. We are all meant to come home to ourselves, even if we find ourselves in environments and cultures that do not necessarily welcome our wholeness. In addition, this process is not meant to be done alone; this is not how it works. Being alone might take us far, but at some point, we need to come back to community. This is what it means to heed the jaguar's call.

EMBODY THE JAGUAR

Your Healing Path

- What has your own path of healing looked like so far? What tools and modalities have you turned to in order to reclaim your body, calm your mind, and bring peace and presence to all parts of yourself?
- Describe any times when you didn't feel at home—in your body, or in the larger culture. What was the primary medicine you counted on to help you locate a sense of "home"? Please be compassionate as you consider whether

you may have "overharvested" this medicine in your search for healing.

- Have there been times when the full scope of your identity and experience of walking through the world felt like it didn't fit into the spiritual teachings you received? For example, perhaps the message that "we are all one" excluded experiences you may have had around being isolated from the larger culture due to identities you hold. What were these experiences like for you? Were you led to form any beliefs?

- When you think of "reconciliation," what kinds of associations does that word bring up? What parts of your own life are you hoping to reconcile with?

2
RECONNECTING WITH NATURE

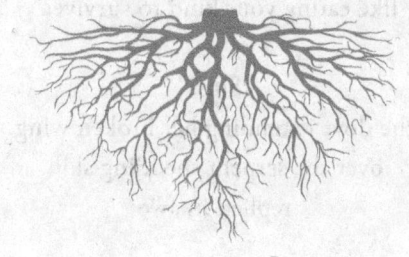

Am I Holy?

"What do I need to be holy?"
asked the serpent to the dove

"Holy?
Oh, beloved one
Holy you are since the day the egg cracked—
don't you remember?"

"How about my sins
like eating your kind to survive?"

"Sins?"
the dove extending her broken wing
over the serpent shedding skin
replied in awe

"Oh beloved one, that is who you are—
eating to survive is part of life
My children were eaten when the
holy oak changed its leaves
There is no sin
for being who you are in the chain of life

The tales of our siblings walking on two feet
trapped us between houses built from wood
into a wilderness of sand-made glass

They took the wild from us
and made stories to justify their crimes

But holy, holy—
I see your holiness from miles away
You are much deserving of grace
like everyone else in this cosmic egg"

The dove with a broken wing bobbed her head
pinned her eyes to the horizon
and flew away

What is our intrinsic holiness? How do we connect to the woven artwork of Nature, which includes the elements, our ancestors, and the blood and bones that constitute our genetic and spiritual history? I began to ask myself these questions through the process of reconciliation. I came to the conclusion that Nature—the fabric of interconnectedness that holds all beings together—is the most stable basis for doing our reconciliation work and tapping into who we truly are.

I am reminded of a time when I was doing tree pose in a yoga studio in the middle of a busy city. I was finding it very difficult to follow the teacher's guidance, which asked that we imagine ourselves as a tree, with our branches reaching into the sky and our roots delving into the earth. It felt too abstract for me—until I looked out the window and saw a very tired, scraggly-looking tree that appeared to be struggling in the midst of this concrete jungle. I suddenly got it. I didn't have to be a great big, sprawling oak; I could be *this* unassuming tree that was simply trying to stay rooted, despite the inhospitable conditions. It was a powerful moment because it gave me an embodied experience of the tree pose. It also offered me a window back into my own culture. In the Andean tradition, we call upon Nature to give us strength, but this is a relationship that requires great reciprocity and respect, as we are engaging in an energetic exchange. I felt this exchange as I embodied that tree outside the yoga studio.

Some part of me has always understood that the process of coming back to myself was, in the broadest sense, inextricable from Nature.

The Earth's many diverse organisms are part of a complex tapestry of life, where everything has its place. I began to realize that whenever I felt divided, I could always come home to myself by rooting back into Nature—which no teacher or culture has a monopoly over . . . and I pray it stays this way for generations to come.

Throughout my life, spending time in Nature has been a vital aspect of attending to my well-being. Whether I am walking on the beach, hiking in the mountains, or simply talking to trees and plants, all these experiences provide a sense of belonging and unconditional love I cannot find elsewhere. Interestingly enough, it wasn't until I moved to an urban environment that I realized just how important Nature was to my well-being.

Early on my healing path, I began engaging in somatic and body-awareness practices, as well as sacred Nature pilgrimages, in order to recover my sense of wellness and freedom. These practices were crucial in helping me find my way back to my physical body and my inner Nature. From there, I expanded my engagement with Nature to include herbal and horticultural therapy—recognizing that these practices were used in many traditions for thousands of years before science labeled and categorized them, evaluated their results and efficacy, and created metrics that made them more available for mass consumption.

With my husband's help, I have cultivated an indoor/outdoor herb garden for years and have over two dozen plants that fill my home office. For more than a decade, my family and I have moved frequently—my husband is in the Navy—and most of my indoor plants have always made the trip with us, no matter where we go. I cook my herbs and make medicinal teas throughout the year. I share some of the most aromatic herb buckets and mixed tea blends with friends in my community.

Through this process, I rediscovered the importance of reconnecting with my Indigenous roots and culture. The people of the Andes have had a profound relationship with Nature for millennia. Even though the environments in which Andean cultures flourished are sometimes harsh, the people have always been resilient. From their architecture to their textiles, from their medical practices to their culinary practices, Andean cultures from their inception were a direct response to the natural environment. They understood the importance of maintaining a reciprocal relationship with Nature and the environment. They understood that caring for outer Nature was a way of being in right relationship with inner Nature. This realization about my roots inspired me to work with people from similar backgrounds, encouraging them to engage with Nature while working together to protect and preserve the natural world. I also teach my clients how to connect with their inner nature, which has a significant impact on their overall health and well-being.

Why is Nature so important in the process of healing? Even if you don't believe in anything in particular, most major religions and belief systems come back to Nature in some form—whether they are rooted in science or in the idea of a "God." And all human experiences are facilitated through the body and our senses, which are connected to Nature. Communing with Nature is a way to connect with the sacred aspect of life, and in many spiritual systems, the elements are seen as mighty Gods or spirits. Nature reminds us of the interconnectedness of all phenomena, which exist in a delicate balance of life and death.

This is also important, because many people might be drawn to a belief system that hails from a specific cultural context and way of life that might be unfamiliar to us. It is so important to consider how the quest for individual healing can unknowingly contribute to the problems of cultural appropriation and what I've already referred to as "overharvesting." A simple example is Ayahuasca, a sacred plant medicine that has been used by the Indigenous people of various regions of the Amazon, including Perú, for centuries and is now beginning to enter the mainstream wellness world. Many Peruvians in urban areas, who have not been acquainted with this sacred medicine, are being reintroduced to Ayahuasca through a Eurocentric mindset—which tends to be focused on individual healing and self-enrichment. Because of ecotourism that has been perpetuated by the influx of people from Western nations, leading to environmental degradation, hundreds of jungle territories have been demolished to make way for resorts and retreat centers that serve the demands of those who do not hail from the region—and who do not come from a long lineage of those who cultivated an intentional relationship with Ayahuasca.

Even an action as seemingly harmless as seeking a medicine that comes from a plant whose ceremonies originated in a specific region of the world can have so many ramifications for the people and for Nature in that part of the world. We can walk with a greater sense of respect for Nature, rather than simply investigating medicines that will comfort us when we feel lost. Yes, Nature will absolutely be there to catch us when we fall, but our relationship with it can never be pure if we are simply using it as a "tool" for our own selfish reasons. While healing is always for your benefit and the benefit of all beings, it is possible for us to weaponize our healing against the natural world, for the sake of "getting what I want."

I invite you, beloved friend, to recognize that Nature is a place of refuge, but it also asks that we bring to it something in return: a gift of reciprocity that demonstrates our understanding of the sacred dance. We can learn so much from Nature when we open ourselves up with humility and a heart that is seeking to understand and to give, rather than only seeking understanding and to take.

We are Nature. Like Nature, we have been exploited, but our fundamental truth is wholeness. Like Nature, we belong to the Earth (matter), and we are also born from the dust of the stars and celestial beings. Like Nature, this fundamental celestial energy can never be taken away. But in order to open up to our full capacities, we have to recognize the places where pain and trauma may have created a sense of numbness or loss—a place where we may be in danger of overharvesting Nature's bounty and goodness.

Think of Nature as the loving grandmother who will place her manta over your shoulders to keep you warm, and who will make you delicious and nourishing food in order to feed your body, mind, and spirit. However, if you cross her or do her wrong, you'll definitely be hearing from her!

This means that when you are healing with Nature, it is a good idea to practice listening. Practice asking permission before you take anything from Nature. For example, if you are foraging on a walk through the forest, ask the herbs, plants, and berries you encounter, as well as the birds and the wind, whether it is right to take anything with you. It may feel awkward at first if you've never done this before—which is true for many of us who've come to live in cultures that do not honor the non-human world but see it as ripe for the picking. Over time, you will begin to understand the way Nature speaks to you: through your own subtle knowing and through signs that come your way.

Accept Nature's yes and gracefully accept her no if you sense she is saying, "Now is not the time." For example, I recall working with a client who shared with me that she'd received a clear message from Ayahuasca that this medicine was no longer for her (and perhaps had never been). Rather than questioning the guidance or making justifications for why she should continue to take it, my client respected what she received and took it as a sign to move on; she was now ready to reconcile with her roots in different ways.

MIRROR THE JAGUAR
Connecting to Nature

- In what ways do you feel connected to Nature? What is your first memory of communing with Nature? How has this changed or remained constant over the years?

- Think about your family of origin or the roots you hail from. What are some of the ways in which your ancestors communed with Nature, especially to promote healing and individual and collective well-being? Please know that you may have to ask your elders or do some research around this, especially if you don't feel directly connected to your lineage or your family didn't pass down many traditions.

- Have you engaged in any behaviors with respect to Nature that have created a sense of imbalance? Please be compassionate as you consider ways you might have unwittingly appropriated, overharvested, or failed to ask permission. For example, I was once on a pilgrimage at a local beach and received a subtle message from my inner being: "You want a souvenir from our encounter? Stop stealing my shells. Instead, pick up the trash that's left by your kind and is floating on my shores, killing your brothers and sisters, the creatures of the sea. Then, display that trash with pride and sorrow."

- Can you commit to opening your heart to a reciprocal and loving relationship with Nature? In what ways can you begin to listen for Nature's guidance? For example, you can pay attention to any messages you intuitively receive on the wind. You can also observe the birds and trees to discern the deeper wisdom of the seasons, and how all beings participate in this dance.

EMBRACING THE ELEMENTS

Throughout this book, I'll be inviting you to come into your own relationship with the elements of Nature—water, wind, fire, and earth—in the way that makes the greatest sense for you. This is one of the most beautiful and effective ways to intentionally work with Nature's healing properties and to create a foundation for your own process of reconciliation.

My association with the elements comes from Pacha philosophy. Water, wind, fire, and earth are connected to the spiritual, social, political, and economic aspects of life, present in cycles of planting, harvest, birth, death, and celebration. Although the elements each symbolize a number of different characteristics, here's how I think about them:

1. Water heals and gives life.
2. Wind carries wisdom and freedom.
3. Fire purifies, transmutes, and regenerates.
4. Earth nurtures and sustains.

Pacha philosophy also tells us about its own consciousness, which can be described as the void. It can be related to the "fifth element," known as ether or space in some systems of thought. This aspect of Pacha is connected to that which does not exist in form. Later in this chapter, I will share my explanation of why I often suggest that people on a path of trauma-related dissociation avoid working directly with this aspect.

Though the elements have medicinal energies, they also have destructive qualities. This is why they need to be held with reverence and in a state of balance; we must not romanticize them. Sometimes, fire burns, water floods the nervous system, earth creates a sense of heaviness and loss of motivation, and wind carries death and sickness. Aside from approaching the elements with great respect, we must always recognize that they might carry their own fair share of trauma with them. For example, the waters brought me healing, but I can't ignore that they also brought the boats and boots of the colonizer to Perú, where I was born.

In addition, we must take into account that our sacred practices with the elements can sometimes be overly rushed, incomplete, or undertaken with the wrong motives and focus. We can work with the elements to balance energy in our lives, but if our sacred practices are not done properly, they can backfire. Over time, in working with the elements, I've learned how to protect myself from the destructive ramifications of not cleansing and transmuting energy in the correct ways. At the same time, I marvel at the power of the elements and also recognize that, sometimes, the sickness carried by the wind or the natural events wrought by the water are necessary in order to take us to the next phase of our journey.

Often, working with the elements requires its own process of reconciliation if we consider that Nature is a force that encompasses gale-force hurricanes and quiet little streams. It is as complex as we are.

Coming into relationship with the elements may feel messy and chaotic, and there will be moments when we contain it in ritual and sacred contracts. Here, beloved friend, I want to emphasize that I prefer the term *sacred contract* to *ceremony*, as it denotes a personal relationship to Pacha that we are affirming by articulating our own requests and responsibilities. There are two parties involved—you and Nature—in a relationship of reciprocity. At the same time, there are precise formats that should be followed in certain sacred-contract contexts and traditions, including Pacha philosophy, that are beyond the scope of this book.

Our connection with Nature and the elements cannot be prescriptive or something that we gain by reading a book. It must be an experiential and relational practice that we develop over time, and through careful observation of and reverence for our natural environment. We must each find our own way to the elements. Although I will be offering ways for you to come into relationship with the elements, the order in which you approach them, as well as *how* you approach them, must be primal, intuitive, and raw. Do not use your "thinking" mind. Remember that as you approach the elements, you are just an essence connecting with another essence and recognizing that you, too, are elemental. Unfortunately, books have historically been used to colonize our cognition and experiences, but the process of coming face to face with the jaguar is as far away from the thinking mind as we can get.

The next section offers some ideas about how you can connect to the elements in your daily life, but I encourage you to sit with what feels best, as well as how your ancestors may have honored the elements.

WATER

There are so many ways to connect with water, although it's worth noting that water is quickly becoming a precious limited resource. Water is life, and it's also true that, throughout history, those who have controlled the wells and waterways have also controlled the flow of life. However, control over water, like control over any aspect of Nature, is a man-made fantasy. This fascinating and potent energy that has the power to give life and nurture all existing life forms can also be formidable and destructive, especially when sacred balance has been broken.

All water comes from somewhere. As you take a shower or bath, be grateful for the privilege of opening your faucet so that pure life force in the form of water can come surging out. Contemplate the many paths the water took—from clouds pregnant with rain to reservoirs to underground wells to the pipes in your house—to get to you. Think of all the processes that occurred in order for it to come your way. As the water covers you, offer it your thanks. If you do not have the privilege of access to running water, you might pour water from a lake or river over your body. As you do this, consider your connection to water. Consider the liquidity and flow of your own blood. Up to 60 percent of the adult human body is made of water. All of this water comes from Mother Earth.

For a more immersive experience (literally), you might wish to dip yourself fully in a body of water. Many spiritual traditions offer processes of cleansing and healing our bodies, minds, and spirits in a river or other body of water. We can always give this body of water any heavy energy (e.g., grief, trauma, despair, etc.) that we want to reconfigure. In fact, in Andean medicine, we feed our heavy energy to Nature, because it is hungry due to many factors, including our overharvesting of its spiritual medicine. However, it doesn't have to be only heavy energy that we give; we can also undertake this process with joy in our hearts—offering a simple breath or prayer that we can lovingly give to Nature's hungry creatures.

WIND

There's a childhood saying I love: "When you walk the path alone, you always have the wind." The wind, of course, contains the oxygen that sustains us and makes respiration possible. Working with intentional breathing can rejuvenate our mental capacities and bring regulation to the mind and body, balancing us and creating calm and equilibrium.

The wind carries weather patterns and fresh new gusts of air. Information travels on the wind and brings to us wisdom, realizations, and knowledge that can stir us into action and help us to understand what we may not have previously understood. By whistling or singing with the birds, we can go beyond the confines of the mind, which might be stubbornly wedded to language, and engage in a call-and-response that takes us into deeper terrain. We might find ourselves playfully sending forth messages in a language we don't even understand, but our energy will be received and carried by the wind.

We can also consider that even the things we do not say can still travel. And when we verbalize them, these words are carried very far on the wind, so we should be conscious of what we are saying. Even if our words may seem to be very private (such as cussing out a driver who cuts us off on the highway), the wind will carry the words we speak and the stories we tell—to the world, to the celestial beings in the upper world, and to the ancestors and other beings in the underworld. As we work with the wind, we can also practice discernment. A profound practice is to offer our hopes and prayers on the wind, consciously choosing our words and intentions, as well as the emotions and sensations with which we infuse them. Doing this can help to manifest a very different reality from the one we may have been previously accustomed to.

FIRE

Fire is an ancient element that existed at the dawn of infinite creation, when the galaxies, stars, and planets formed through explosions of intense heat. Fire brings us closer to our physical Nature. There can be no life without fire. The fire of the Sun catalyzes all of life, and the heat produced by our cells and metabolic processes fills us with vitality and health. The spark of our inner fire that regenerates our intentions, motivations, and our passion is also what sustains us in this life. Fire can be the element that gives us an extra blaze of inspiration and the wherewithal to fulfill our dreams and move through adversity.

We can connect with fire in a variety of simple ways, such as rubbing our palms together to feel our intrinsic warmth and vitality, while offering gratitude and praise to that force that maintains our internal and external spark. This is a wonderful way to feel both our physical aliveness and to honor our inner fire. Another invigorating way to work with fire can be writing a letter with or without words—you can use scrawls, lines, symbols, and anything that expresses who you are as a primal being—about what you wish to transmute, and then burning it. Fire has both a purifying and destructive property, and just as water can wash away the stagnant energy we are carrying, fire can consume and change that which disrupts harmony and balance, while remembering that sometimes, what appears not to serve us may be fulfilling a purpose we are not aware of. As the smoke travels on the wind, it carries our intention of letting go of the old and welcoming in the new.

EARTH

The earth stabilizes and grounds us, offering a sense of connection to this living realm and all its diverse forms. In Pacha philosophy, the general worldview tends to be agriculturally-centric, both in the way we consider relations with the natural world and in the way we "earth" our own spiritual nature. Earth is an element that is associated with cultivating, growing, and nurturing the life that is all around us. When we work with the earth element, we honor Nature in all her forms. From the way we fertilize the soil to the way we care for the plants and trees that grow from that soil, working with earth is all about honoring life through all its cycles—and never taking more than what is required for our own sustenance.

Many people who live in the Western world don't know where our food comes from. We go to the grocery store and purchase items that are created by corporations that are more interested in yielding a profit than caring for people. Products are often churned out at a low cost, with questionable ingredients and little attention paid to the environmental impact of perpetual growth and constant consumption. Honoring the earth element can entail learning more about sustainability. If you eat meat, consider how the livestock you are consuming were raised. How were the animals treated? It's also a good idea to learn where your produce comes from. Overall, knowing the source of your food and supporting organic local and small farmers who raise their food humanely and with care for the environment helps you to make responsible and healthy choices.

I personally enjoy observing root vegetables and produce that grow inside the earth. It's a wonderful thing to care for the seeds of the vegetables we consume and prepare them for planting in the next season. I like to let a potato sit for a few weeks and contemplate the sprouts that come out of it, as they remind me of the way I am always connected to the planet, through my own metaphorical root system. Another way I like to connect with the earth element is to walk without shoes, expressing gratitude to the Earth for the wholeness of my body. Honoring the earth as sacred by making reverential, full-body contact with it can also be a wonderful way to touch the ground of our being and to feel connected to the natural world.

THE CONSCIOUSNESS OF PACHA

The consciousness of Pacha is the essence of time, space, emptiness, and the void from which all the other elements emerged. Some schools of thought will refer to this as the "fifth element," but that isn't really accurate in Pacha philosophy. It is a difficult phenomenon to describe because it is ineffable—it lives beyond our human comprehension, even though we may attempt to lock it inside categories and language.

The consciousness of Pacha is the phenomenon of the celestial realm, where all things originated and continue to be sustained. It is Pacha in and of itself. There is no time, space, or matter here. The place of this mystical aspect is where relationality, complementarity, correspondence, reciprocity, and cyclicality begin—and simultaneously, it transcends all of this. But it isn't necessarily the best place for us—because we live in human bodies! Our role isn't to leave our bodies and soar with metaphorical condors; it is to be human, which means that we must tend to and care for Nature and matter. It is to remain in the realm of the jaguar, to really be *here*. I know it can be easy for some to be out there, but we need you here. Your medicine is for the *Kay Pacha*, or "the place of humans and matter." I have met people who insist that they feel they were dropped on Earth from another planet or star system and that they don't belong here, but as I have observed, this can be a way for a person to turn away from the messy business of being human and a sign that they may be dealing with wounding that has not yet been addressed.

Of course, all of us are part of Nature, and we contain all of the elements. The Judeo-Christian religions say we were all made in God's image, but this can create a false association with power. We might come to believe that we *are* Gods! This is true on a more absolute and universal level, but it can also be abused to claim a sense of superiority over others, and over Nature itself. Yes, we are divine beings, but in my daily life, I don't live as if I am the goddess of the moon or ocean. I live like I am the legs of the jaguar and the manta of my *abuelita*, (a Spanish term of endearment that's similar to "Granny").

In many spiritual circles, I have also witnessed a tendency for people to insist that the goal of life is to be "one with the universe." This can be a beautiful concept, but where is our core? It must be connected to something tangible, because that is the plane of existence where we, and the jaguar, live. If we insist on being too elevated and too ethereal, we lose perspective and sustainability. We might even come to oppress other living beings in our desire to feel almighty, when perhaps we should be more interested in feeling the holiness of the tree who is struggling to survive, or the sacredness of a mountain in the valley that's being exploited for its precious gems and divvied up to create more dwelling places for people.

Overall, relying solely on the ethereal world can be a shortcut—a way to avoid doing the important human labor to grow ourselves and the world. According to Pacha philosophy, it is our responsibility as humans to breed, in the broadest sense of the word: to nurture, to create, to plant, and to propagate. We must breed not only families and communities but ourselves, as we seek to grow and build a symbiotic connection with nature. Ironically, connecting to the consciousness of Pacha doesn't have to mean leaving our bodies and communing with otherworldly realms. To connect with the celestial realm, we can simply be present with the elements, so that when and if the consciousness of Pacha decides to manifest to us, our body and mind can be a robust vessel for receiving its messages.

Remember, the purpose of working with the elements, of reconciling with Nature, of healing our own disconnection, is to offer us the capacity to be conduits for communal wellness. This means that we must not try to escape our embodied experience; rather, we must root more intentionally into it, as this will help us to move with integrity and a sense of responsibility to ourselves and the planet.

TENDING TO LOOSE THREADS IN THE MANTA

As I've already mentioned, I have a loving relationship with the waters of rivers, particularly the areas where the sweet water of the river meets the salty waters of the ocean. In recent years, I have been fortunate enough to travel extensively throughout Central and South America for work, and to research and compile ancient wisdoms. One of the most rewarding things to do when I get to traditional towns and villages and share with the community is to listen to stories from the elders of the towns. During one of my visits to the land of the Boruca, the Indigenous people of Costa Rica, an elder mentioned that the river that runs through its mountains and touches the ocean has its own journey, just like any one of us.

One day, my crew and I were ready to jump on a little boat and set sail downstream. Luck had it that the jungle started talking and began pouring down rain. The captain of the little boat, a native Boruca fisherman, told us that while it was safe for us to go, it would be better to trust my gut. Standing there under the rain with the desire to cross the river to the Pacific Ocean, something inside me said to wait until the rain passed. In the moment, there was imprinted in my heart and mind the image of the little boat leaving the mangroves to face open waters, the impact of each wave against the metal, the breeze transforming from sweet to salty, the boat suspended in the air as it suffered the waves, and the seemingly smooth and deep-brown river water fighting to integrate with the vastness of the ocean. So we waited.

The next day, because of the heavy rain there was a high tide, and the waters were very rocky. On the previous day when nature had shown me its greatness and fury, I had received the message that I felt in my gut of what was to come, just like my fisherman captain mentioned.

That is what reintegration and reconciliation mean. I saw with my spiritual eyes my own experience and the rocky, messy, and, at times, fearful and magical journey of reconciling the fragmented parts of myself. From that moment forward, when life throws me a curveball and I disassociate from my body, mind, and situation, I go back to the images of the river reconnecting with the ocean, where fresh and salt water belong to each other.

My sense of gradual reconnection with water, my primary element, was messy and difficult. This is likely to be true for many of us, but the pathway toward reconciliation through the elements is a powerful one that brings us into a more complete relationship with ourselves and the natural world. It makes us more capable of holding the paradoxes of our life, just as I held the sweet waters of the river with the salt waters of the ocean.

I also recently had a profound relationship with the element of fire. The fire that had moved within me for years was young, tender, and rebellious. I'd been brought up in survival mode, and my fire was used in service of helping me to move swiftly and purposefully through rough times. However, during a sacred contract assisted by the breath, I felt the presence of an ancient, wise, and powerful forebear Fire. I heard this fire tell me, "You found yourself through the water. Then, you followed your wind—and on your wind, the breath, I am now revealing myself to you. Your fire is ancient, and its roots run very deep, just like the volcanoes rising from the depths of the Pacific Ocean. You can continue to count on me—your older fire—by paying attention to the wind. But remember, when there is too little of me, I dry up. And if there is too much of me, I burn you and everything else."

It was an astounding and insightful moment. I had consistently related so much to water, but now fire was offering me a portal through which I could discover new parts of myself. I felt that this fire was telling me it was time to move beyond survival mode and into flourishing.

The elements came to me almost as loving parents or grandparents. They helped me to reconnect with myself. However, what often stands in the way of our relationship to Nature is a sense of disconnection from ourselves—not just from our individual power and potential, but from a sense of rootedness within a supportive culture that steers us to be a part of a larger fabric.

This disconnection is at the root of something I believe many of us in this era of humanity are dealing with: the grief of not feeling the presence of grace in our lives. Grace, for many, might have a religious connotation, but it is beyond that. Grace is inherent to who we are; it is the experience of knowing our intrinsic worth because we are part of Nature and part of the elements. Grace is always present, because it is woven into our essence. But when we feel alone, isolated, and lacking the support of our relatives, communities, and the larger world, we become like loose threads in the manta. Grace helps us to know that we are already a part of the manta—but when we question this, we experience a sense of uprootedness and disorientation that makes it difficult to see our own lives as sacred.

There are people inhabiting this world feeling disconnected, as if they don't understand or like it here. There are others who are like me—far from the land of their ancestors, where they might have also experienced cultural trauma, and re-planted in places that at times, feel inhospitable. Then, there are those who were adopted or fostered, and have no access to their biological family and ancestral roots. There are also those who are disconnected from their lineage due to assimilation, as well as those whose lineage includes forced migration, such as indentured servitude and slavery. We also have the increasingly common case of refugees who were separated from the land in which their seed and the seeds of their ancestors grew, due to war and other conflict. Some people who experience the grief of living in a state of estrangement still live on the land of their ancestors, but it has been stolen from them or abused—which is the plight of so many Indigenous people around the world. In addition, people who appear to live a privileged life but lack connection to the Earth and don't know how to care for Nature might also experience the grief of not feeling grace . . . of being cut off from the manta of life.

The consequences of being cut off from the manta, of not knowing that we are grace embodied, is that we might act out in not-so-holy ways. There are, of course, those who have done a great deal of damage to others and to the planet. It might be difficult to see them as suffering, but they are. We suffer when we are fragmented and disconnected from an awareness of our true source. This can also be true for people who continue to be the beneficiaries of their ancestors' conquest of different parts of the world, even though it might be easy to deny accountability or wrongdoing. In truth, we inherit the pain, suffering, and wrongdoing of our ancestors, and through our own reconciliation process, we can put right what was taken out of balance. But when we fail to do this, it is as if we are fruits that fell off a tree without ripening. We suffer, often without realizing the source of our suffering.

The good news is Nature can be a mother or grandmother to all of us. And in truth, we need all of us—spiritual orphans to be nurtured back to wholeness and grace—because all of us belong to one another, and to the weaving fabric of this living multiverse.

Beloved friend, no matter who you are or where your life began, you may have felt this experience of being orphaned, bereft of connection and a sense of rootedness. I certainly found myself in that state for a number of years. My hope is that this book will be like the caring mother or grandmother who constitutes all of Nature. She, too, has been hurt, rejected, and abused, but she still carries her warm manta that she is eager to drape over your shoulders. She is still capable of caring for others. And as you heal, you will build your own capacity to care for those who are similarly in search of healing. For when we experience our own wholeness, we cannot help but blanket everything around us with it.

But you also have a responsibility here. Nature will be here for you, to weave you back into the inherent grace, strength, and power you truly hold within yourself . . . but you must also be here for her. You must also do your part in engaging with her, responsibly and with the intention to be a steward of healing on this enchanting planet.

EMBODY THE JAGUAR
Elemental Sacred Contracts

- What is the element you feel the deepest connection to? Consider the natural environment of your ancestors, as well as the place or terrain in which you grew up. What were some of the primary landforms and natural phenomena (rivers, oceans, mountains, forests, and winds)? This may also give you a clue as to which element you are naturally drawn to. Please remember that none of the elements are "independent." Nature operates interdependently, and no part is bigger or better than another, but most of us are likely to feel a special bond with one element in particular. For me, that's water.

- What is the element that is calling to you right now? It might not be the same as the element you feel the deepest connection to.

- If you are having difficulty identifying an element that feels right to work with right now, go for the one that feels the most maternal to you—the one that has a nurturing, receptive, welcoming energy. There will be moments when we will know which element to work with because we need to call in a specific quality associated with that element. But for now, move in the direction of the mother. You will know her when you feel her.

- In your own way, and with the use of the elements, especially the one you feel the strongest connection to, create a sacred contract for connecting with Nature and asking for its support. What can you offer as your own commitment to building a relationship with Nature? For example, perhaps you might start volunteering with your local environmental society or begin planting seeds of the native trees in your region.

 Sample: Name of rivers, oceans

 Sample: Name of sacred fires
Name of volcanoes
Sunrise & sunset

 Sample: Name of winds (Santa Ana)
Name of songs or melodies

 Sample: Name of forest
Name of mountains

 Sample: Name of space ecosystems
Aurora Borealis
Meteor showers

Reconnecting with nature means identifying the elements—water, fire, wind, earth, and space—as they manifest in landforms, ecosystems, and ancestral environments. By exploring rivers, forests, and cosmic phenomena, we rediscover our roots and uncover which elements nurture us, guiding us during life's pivotal moments.

3

UNDERSTANDING THE WOUND

Steps "K" and "A" of KARE: Knowing and Assessing Your Wounds

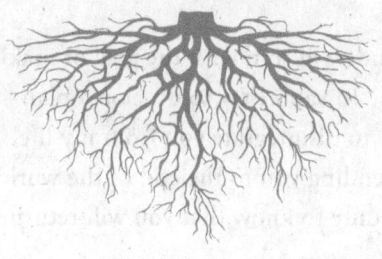

Spending Time with You

I see you,
I feel you,
it's impossible to try to avoid you
because the moment I close my eyes
you are there,
sitting in the background of layered skin
burning from the inside out.

Allowing me a moment to stay with you
may give me the answers to why you
appear in the first place—
and then what?

The clouds will spin with the goal of making rain.
In vain, I try to develop a plan
to disintegrate you from my life,
sending you to the end of the world,
only to know that you will return.

It's unusual to spend time with you
because I don't like you
yet we belong together,
and for the next endless breath,
I will sit at your edge and be with you
while you share your secrets of life.

Oh, pain of mine,
messenger of tears,
sweet reminder of impermanence.

I'm closing my eyes this morning
to spend time with you and dance until the music
finds its way to pregnant clouds
and the rain showers my earthly body.

Oh, pain of mine,
I'm spending time with you
to remember how divinity
opens its wings and shelters me.

I learned to shield my grief and anger in the face of unfairness in order to remain safe. I learned to adapt to a torn society that saw me as "less than." I came to fear being in environments where embodying who I was would push others to undervalue me. I learned to thrive within a system that sells opportunities for success, but lets many drift through dark waters when their services are no longer needed. I learned to live overlooked; to accept mistreatment and abuse in interpersonal relationships. I learned to lick my wounds and pretend everything was okay; to keep my head up and play the part of "strong, resilient woman," all the while knowing this wasn't my complete self.

Most people have experienced feeling alone, hopeless, and "less than," to some degree or another. The fear that gets imprinted into our bodies from past wounds can continue to echo through our daily experiences, even when we are not aware of it.

I grew up in the 1980s in Perú, in a violent environment in which civil war and resource scarcity for some groups were the norm. I still remember the terror brought on by the constant onslaught of deafening bombs and open fire. But fear compelled something else, too. My hopelessness in the face of unfair treatment turned into rage; it became the steam my train needed in order to keep moving. Today, I can see my wounds, but I don't live from them. They're a sacred reminder of where I came from and what I endured. But I am done surviving. I am now thriving.

Today, I understand that what I experienced was trauma. According to Pacha philosophy, my nuna went running. Because many of us are forced into survival mode by our life circumstances, we learn to bury our trauma and create a persona—something that is especially true for re-planted people, and those underrepresented in the larger culture. This sense of a double mentality—of navigating two different realities or parts of one's identity at the same time—is an aspect of my resilience, but it also served to disconnect me from my lived experiences. I didn't recognize until years later that it was also causing my wound to bleed more acutely.

While trauma is becoming a buzzword in the modern world, we are only beginning to understand the impact and trauma around migration and acculturation. Along with the feeling of not fully belonging that re-planted people are often subjected to, they also often feel pressured to cut off parts of themselves because they are led to believe that where they come from is "less than" the society in which they re-plant themselves.

Many re-planted people deal with trauma that occurs before, during, and after the re-planting process. Unfortunately, these aspects are often rendered invisible in conversations about trauma and PTSD as we currently know them—without taking into account their own long-standing protocols to deal with wounding. All of this is why we'll spend some time talking about why our social and cultural context is such an important part of understanding the wounds we carry, and what it takes to properly treat them.

Regardless of our background, most of us have undergone trauma, and understanding the nature of our wounds is critical to reconciling with our roots and reclaiming our wholeness. You may be familiar with your own suffering, but it's also true that many of us have been disconnected from the full effects of our pain and trauma—especially if we have been doing what we need to in order to survive and make our way through a world that was not designed for our thriving.

If the idea of digging into your wounds is daunting, please know that you're not alone. Maybe you, like me and many people in this world, grew up in a dysfunctional family that sagged beneath the weight of intergenerational trauma. Maybe you went through a massive change later in your life that still haunts you. Possibly, you have been hurt in ways that you cannot even articulate. Perhaps you still hold the pain of those conscious and unconscious memories with you, and over the years, they've snowballed into a larger pain that became the invisible weight you now carry with you.

My hope is that the information in this chapter will not overwhelm you but will serve as a guide that validates your experiences and brings you into acceptance of yourself as you are. An important tool in the healing process is the KARE method. KARE is an acronym where K stands for knowing and identifying your wound; A stands for assessing the dimensions of the breakage; R stands for reconciling what is out of order; and E stands for engendering ongoing remedies for healing. In this chapter, we'll go slow and work with the first two parts of KARE: *knowing* and *assessing*.

Contrary to popular belief, I want you to know there is nothing to fix or change, beloved one. The events of your life have made you who you are, and they include your strengths. But if you want to get to a place of greater clarity, openness, and connection to your deepest roots, at some point you will have to investigate where in your body the emotional charge—from being neglected, overlooked, abused, betrayed—resides and continues to operate.

I see you, I hear you, I love you.

TRAUMA FROM A MULTIDIMENSIONAL PERSPECTIVE

There are many definitions of trauma that pass in and out of vogue, especially as we move into a more "trauma-informed" awareness in the realm of personal development, therapy, mind/body wellness, and spirituality. I see trauma as a download that impacts our software (our inner coding/programming) and has an immediate effect on our hardware (our body, which is our interface with the world around us).

Trauma can be the body's response to events that overwhelm us, leaving us unable to cope with the impact of circumstances, such as neglect or abuse from our caregivers when we were children. It can also come from painful memories, both recent and distant, such as being in the midst of war and turmoil, or encountering accidents and natural events.

It might also entail debilitating feelings of inadequacy that linger long after these experiences, or the constant reminder that we are less than human because of how the world sees us—perhaps as migrants or refugees who dared to re-plant elsewhere, or as people born LGBTQ+ or with different skin tones or differently abled bodies. Trauma's reverberations run through every aspect of our lives, including how we size up a situation or person to determine whether we are safe. And while there may be situations where we *aren't* safe, trauma wields a knife that cuts through our ability to see, feel, and sense our surroundings with clarity and accuracy. However, when we develop a relationship with the body and the truth of the present moment, we can start to interpret what is happening for us. The body is the first actor in the trauma play. Before our psychology can make sense of what's going on, the body can immediately tell. It is truly the map of our experience.

Trauma is so painful because it separates us from the core of who we are. We forget that we came into this world with eternal grace. The spark that brought us to life is nothing but pure consciousness. It is beyond good or bad, wrong or right; it is simply a neutral manifestation of deep wisdom. And I'm not even talking about something mystical! Science has already given us evidence that we're made of the same material as the primordial matter of the universe. But when our software is altered and our hardware is tampered with, this impacts our self-image and how we think about and navigate life.

Let me bring these concepts to a living embodied experience. For years, one of my clients, Rosa, felt like she was the monster in her own movie. She felt disjointed and awkward in her body, and it was impossible to be at home inside her own skin. She also thought of her parents with an enormous amount of resentment and hostility—for they were the ones who were responsible for the monster.

Rosa had experienced brutal neglect at the hands of her caregivers, and she'd been at the whims of the US foster-care system, which embedded the idea in her that, as a brown-skinned female, she was worthless, unwanted, and at the bottom of the barrel. She did exactly what many people do in the face of pain; she pulled herself up by the bootstraps and became a fighter. On the outside, Rosa was a successful attorney, but her success was her armor against the world. Her inner life was like a series of fogged funhouse mirrors that she navigated in terror, alone.

When I met her, she told me she'd been struggling with endometriosis, a chronic disease that caused her prolonged pain and body-wide systemic issues. Aside from difficult periods, she was at risk of facing long-term reproductive issues and other related and challenging conditions.

Rosa also shared with me that she felt like "Frankenstein's monster"—not a whole being, but stitched together in ugly, contorted ways. Few people knew about the deep pain that Rosa carried, because the picture she presented to the world was of a confident, outgoing, beautiful woman. Not even her partner was aware of the deep shame she carried over being abandoned by her parents, which had come to exacerbate her physical experience. Rosa had become an expert pretender, walking around with the double mentality that so many trauma survivors harbor.

It's true that we cover our "stitches" and wounds with all kinds of things, from material success to clothing and makeup, in order to fit into our society and culture. Rosa had some sense of this, as she opened up to me about her experience over time.

One of the things Rosa and I worked through as she came to familiarize herself with her wound was her sense that she was constantly being victimized by others. Rosa described feeling triggered by the words, actions, and smallest gestures of the people around her. I completely understand that those of us who have experienced trauma may feel like we're navigating a world full of landmines that could explode at any moment. However, it's important to recognize that we live in an era that has made us hyper-alert. We're saturated with information and stimulation, and it's inevitable that we'll be triggered by something that occurs in our environment, either inadvertently or because someone is trying to get a reaction out of us. The goal of working through our wounds is *not* to avoid being triggered or to demonize other people for triggering us. Instead, we must be willing to face the jaguar with unapologetic truth and radical intimacy; that is, we must recognize what triggers us, get curious, and learn how to respond in skillful ways.

I guided Rosa to identify and access her own inner resources—all those activities, places, people, situations, and ways of being that would help her tap into the embodied experiences of safety, especially when she *didn't* feel safe.

I want to emphasize here that what I refer to as "embodied experiences" is better described as *sentipensante*, a Spanish term that translates to "sensing/thinking," in which we acknowledge that the processes of the mind and heart are not separate, and that thinking and feeling occur simultaneously. This is the process through which we put thought and feeling together; it is the fusion of two ways of perceiving and interpreting reality, based on reflection and emotional connection, until they converge in the same experience of knowledge and action. This helps us to step outside of the tendency to frame our thoughts and feelings as somehow disconnected, and it gives us a greater capacity to connect with our wholeness.

Because Rosa is a Latina who was raised in both Latin American and Euro-Western society, I recognized that she needed a multidimensional, culturally sensitive approach to her wounding. Unfortunately, many methods of working with trauma are not culturally sensitive. For example, at an early age, I was taught that silence was a way to stay safe and keep myself out of the hands of terrorists in my home country. So, when a meditation teacher asked me to go into silence as a way of being at peace with myself, I had a totally different association with silence that was not necessarily about peace. As I came to discover my inner resources, it actually became easier to transform my associations with silence, so that it could become a refuge. But first, I had to reconnect with my sovereignty by locating a sense of agency and identifying the things that actually *did* elicit greater peace and well-being in my mind and body.

As I worked with Rosa, we started in a simple way. I asked her, "What are some of the basic things you can practice or turn to when you're in distress?" We learned that a cup of tea or a warm blanket draped around her shoulders was enough to soften the influence of the amygdala—the part of the brain that processes our emotions and can also lead to disruptive physical and emotional symptoms when we feel fearful. We also explored somatic approaches and primal embodiment, like focusing on her body and her breath and helping her to release any wilder expressions—including sounds, untamed and free movements, etc.

Somatic approaches acknowledge that traumatic experiences get stuck in our bodies on a cellular level. In fact, our ancestors knew this! Their dances and activities engaging the body are proof of their sophisticated awareness. At the same time, Rosa and I had to inch our way into these methods because her body didn't feel safe enough just yet. However, we learned that when she was a child, she loved listening and dancing to different forms of Latin music; in fact, this was one of her rare memories of feeling happy and carefree when she was young. Together, we created a playlist of songs that supported her to connect to those early sensations of feeling at home in her body.

Of course, many of us are not like Rosa, whose later advantages in life helped her to seek important support in the form of therapy and other resources that would bolster her sense of inner safety. I have met people who are imprisoned, in the throes of debilitating illness or addiction, or in financial hardship. Regardless of these situations, it is still possible to access our innermost resources. For example, there are many cases of incarcerated people who find ways to reconcile with their past actions, to forgive themselves, and to acknowledge that underneath what led them to such a fate is a bedrock of grace and strength. But before they can reach this kind of freedom, many of them have to turn to the Divine, or to something bigger than themselves.

When we hit rock bottom and most forms of consolation and refuge are absent, we can rely on the source. This isn't about looking up to some distant hierarchical God who lives far *above* us; rather, it is about turning inward, to the innate grace that lives *inside* us. The moment we're up against the wall, that's when we know who our God is. We know who we can call upon with all our heart and longing. This gives us the strength to face the jaguar.

MIRROR THE JAGUAR
Feeling the Wound

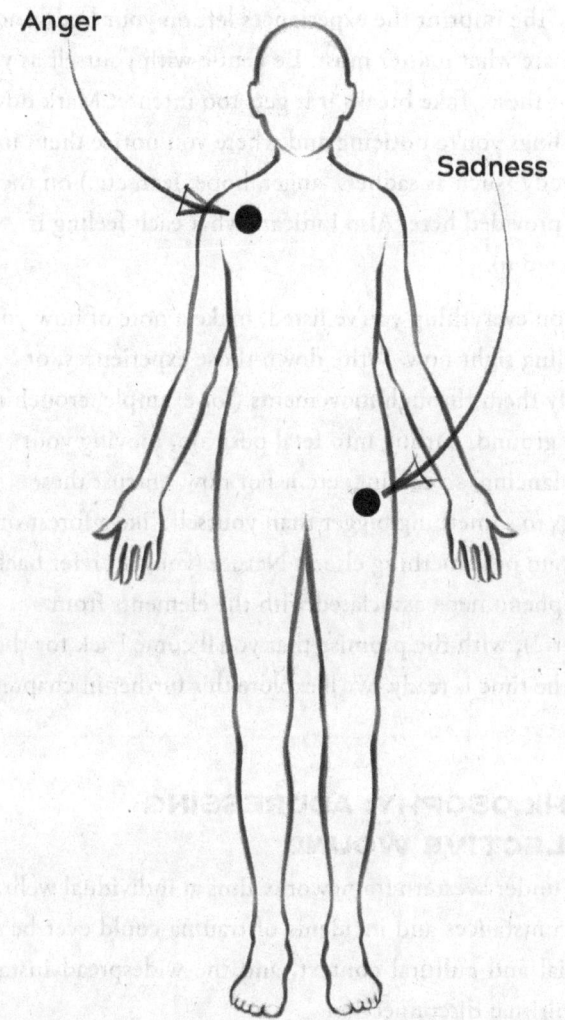

Our physical body holds the imprints of significant life experiences, storing emotions like sadness, anger, hope, etc. in specific areas. By mapping where these feelings reside in the body, we begin the journey of reconnecting with ourselves and others, opening a pathway to healing and integration.

- What are the major experiences in your life that have left a residue of pain and made you feel disconnected from yourself and others? Don't worry so much about the "magnitude" of what you went through as it may appear to others. The imprint the experiences left on your body and psyche are what matter most. Be gentle with yourself as you recount these. Take breaks if it gets too intense. Mark down the feelings you're noticing and where you notice them in your body (such as sadness, anger, hope, fear, etc.) on the image provided here. Also indicate what each feeling is connected to.

- Based on everything you've listed, make a note of how you are feeling right now. Write down those experiences, or embody them through movements (for example, crouching on the ground, curling into fetal position, moving your body, dancing, screaming, etc.). For now, entrust these feelings to something bigger than yourself, like a forest or mountain or something else in Nature (you can refer back to the phenomena associated with the elements from chapter 2), with the promise that you'll come back for them when the time is ready. We'll explore this further in chapter 4.

PACHA PHILOSOPHY: ADDRESSING THE COLLECTIVE WOUND

Most therapy under Western frameworks aims at individual wellness—as if our life circumstances and incidents of trauma could ever be isolated from our social and cultural context, and the widespread instances of human and spiritual disconnection.

Being raised amid Latin American cultural structure, I have firsthand experience with the idea that treating our wounding and early conditioning with the help of community is extremely healing, empowering, impactful, and cost-effective. In the Western world, this may be frowned upon, as it might be considered unconventional to do any kind of trauma work without the proper container or credentials. However, therapy is often not available or accessible to the masses, and we need healing modalities that precede modern psychology and that magnify our innate nature, which is to support and sustain one another. To the best of our ability, we are meant to alternate between being the healers and the ones being healed.

In Pacha philosophy, our wounds and our subsequent healing take place in a collective context. Sickness is thought of as a breakage or disruption in our natural balance. This means that sickness is not just about the individual, but about the ripple effects on an ecosystem when even a small part of it has been knocked off balance. Collective wellness is just as important as individual healing; one can't function without the other.

Often, "therapeutic protocols" are about following a set of prescribed guidelines. I find this is not the most effective way to heal individual and collective maladies. As a trained therapist, I choose not to box myself into a narrow way of serving others. I am a Pacha philosopher and spiritual psychologist—*Nuna Kamayuq* in Quechua. A Nuna Kamayuq is a specialist who knows how to safeguard and steward the sentipensante of another, and who cuts away at the debris surrounding someone's journey. Their work comes from the depths of their experience and their capacity for accompaniment.

A Nuna Kamayuq understands that "anxiety" and "depression" are not new; these are current terms for afflictions of the mind, body, and heart, but they have existed for eons. Our contemporary approaches to mental health are helpful for many people seeking to understand their experiences, but we can also turn to the knowledge and wisdom that's been around for generations to understand ways of addressing our wounding that go beyond pharmaceuticals or talk therapy. Contemporary methods can be effective, but there are many other methods that are just as effective—and that are suitable for people from multicultural backgrounds.

Many of us from multicultural backgrounds come from collectivist traditions. The individualistic mentality of Western culture, though, often creates a false hierarchy that places humans above Nature. However, it's possible to integrate these seemingly opposing approaches. I once heard a story that says that when the experience of the European people connects with the strong will of Anglo-North American people and the devoted love of Latin-American people, true balance in this plane of existence will be possible.

According to an Andean prophecy, the loving and willpower heart of humanity (munay in Quechua) specifically lives in the people of the colonized Americas, whose ability to alchemize emotions will bring the world into balance. And we certainly cannot forget the people on the other side of the world—in Africa and Asia—who have worked since ancient times with powerful methods of managing the mind and body.

In much of Western culture, the new authorities are medical doctors, scientists, psychologists, anthropologists, lawyers, and economists—the widely considered custodians of truth and "objectivity" who have created systems and methodologies based on mental constructs. Pacha philosophy emphasizes a deep connection between the body, nature, and spirituality and it is visceral in content; its methodologies are rooted in balance and loving reciprocity—especially our heart. When it comes down to it, the work of healing the broken heart is the work of engaging munay. We do this sacred work when we move toward wholeness, union, and integration of all our parts.

In fact, Pacha philosophy is not about separating the mind, body, and heart from each other, as they cannot truly be separated. Instead, it's about nourishing the responses of the heart and seeking radical intimacy with the self, for and with community. There's a focus on breaking paradigms of egocentrism, which can further perpetuate trauma, and restoring communal wellness. This approach feeds beautifully into the idea of every individual being both healer and healed.

When we work to heal our wounds from the inside out, we are no longer dependent on limited protocols that emerge from the famous Cartesian split between the mind and body. When we recognize that every individual is part of a collective, and that this collective belongs to Nature, we journey on the path to nourishing and protecting our mental health and sovereignty, and dismantling frameworks that place the thinking mind above the wise, feeling heart. Here, we pay homage to the motherly aspect of Nature and its capacity to tenderly care for us; this is the highest expression of mothering, and it is one that we partake in when we seek to bring ourselves back into balance with community. Like loving mothers, we celebrate together—and we also weep and mourn together. While many of us have experienced wounding at the hands of other people, the paradox is that we also experience healing when our individual threads are drawn back into the manta of interconnectedness.

A Nuna Kamayuq is the spiritual intercessor between humans and unseen forces and they can be sought out to mediate the relationship between an individual and Pacha itself. They also can be relied on to decode spiritual messages, read between the lines, and request balance. I know many Nuna Kamayuq folks who don't have advanced degrees, but they do have a gift for taking people from their misery by restoring a sense of autonomy and sincerely demonstrating to each individual that they are important, loved, and worthy of healing.

While there are numerous therapeutic approaches to understanding and working with the wounds we carry, I appreciate the work of Ignacio Martín-Baró. He was the founder of liberation psychology, which offers an elegant framework for supporting people rooted in Central America. It bears many resemblances to the ancient notion of caring for community that is such a big part of Andean psychology and Pacha philosophy.

We can learn to contextualize our wounds beyond an individual pathology. Understanding the sociocultural, political, historical dimension of our wounding is liberating, because it doesn't trap us in the misunderstanding that it's all our fault, or that we must find our way out of our wounds in isolation from others.

Taking a multicultural approach to mental health means we don't have to compartmentalize our lives by going to a therapist's office when we want to be heard. As I learned from a young age, we go to the *esquina* (corner), *mercado* (marketplace), or *parque* (park) to find our *comadres* and *compadres* (trusted friends/confidants).

Can you imagine what it would be like for teachers and counselors to exhibit a sense of communal care with all their clients? What would it feel like to be offered a space to freely talk about your concerns? To have someone lovingly wrap you in their manta and provide you with a cup of tea? To recognize that someone truly wants to know who you are, and to deeply love you? This is something I wish for you to experience firsthand, beloved friend, if it has not been your experience. In clinical terms, this approach could put a therapist in noncompliance, due to matters of privacy, ethics, and the dangers associated with clients forming unduly strong attachments. However, I have found it to be very effective when it comes to tackling issues that have been hanging out in the shadows for years.

I invite you, beloved friend, to investigate whether you view your own healing as individual or collective. When you experience loneliness and isolation, please remember that each of us is naturally called to community and interconnectedness. So, how can you create space in which you and others feel nurtured and cared for?

THE KARE METHOD: A PROCESS OF VALIDATING THE SELF

In order to understand your wounding and to do the profound work of restoring munay, you must not merely face the jaguar—you must *become* the jaguar. With courage, radical intimacy, and unapologetic truth, you must be willing to patch and sew the fragmented parts of your manta, with reverence and in conjunction with the elements. The healing process is nothing if not active. Even when you are seemingly passive, you're doing something! My work with my clients is all about giving them steps to nurture and care for themselves, and to cultivate a sense of responsibility and agency when it comes to their healing process. This is what I call the "self-breeding process" of Pacha philosophy, because we are always in the process of nourishing and raising ourselves, honoring our autonomy as well as our interdependence with nature.

Although healing is nonlinear and may very well take the remainder of our lives, we learn to be with all parts of ourselves when we take time to understand our wounds. In our modern world, many of us are swinging up and down on the pendulum of healing, between full-on denial/erasure of our suffering and the tendency to actively live inside it so that it colors every aspect of our existence and spills into all our interactions.

I have woven together a system that integrates many different disciplines I've worked with over the years. I often use it with my clients when it comes to assisting them to be radically intimate with the full reality of their wounds, instead of skipping over them. As mentioned earlier, I call this method KARE. And as I described before, this is an acronym that stands for:

- *knowing* and identifying the wound, and recognizing that something happened, which translates to seeing the jaguar

- *assessing* the dimensions of the breakage (of the heart, harmony, balance, etc.), which gives us clarity on what is behind the wound, as well as its impact on our life, which allows us to evaluate our relationship with the jaguar

- *reconciling* what is out of order and calling our nuna back to integrate with the self, which can be likened to meeting the jaguar

- *engendering* ongoing remedies to breed our own healing, well-being, and reconciliation with our nuna—which is akin to embodying the jaguar's coat and legs

Please note that with the KARE method, you may find that you need to be in the K stage for a good length of time. Use the system as you see fit. The framework isn't meant to give you step-by-step instructions down to the detail, but to provide guidance for experimentation, depending on where you are in your healing. An important aspect of healing is cultivating the autonomy to create your own way of working with any resources you are given, so feel free to be nonlinear or to adapt the framework to your unique circumstances and intuition.

Each step of KARE gives us an impactful way of entering a place of compassionate self-witnessing and deep attentiveness that engages our multidimensionality and sentipensante. It asks us to dance between loving and protecting our wounds, and offering companionship—in the way that a mother might care for her child before eventually letting go and allowing the child to explore on their own.

We'll explore the reconciling and engendering processes in greater depth in chapters 4 and 5, but first, let's dive into the first two aspects of this framework: knowing (seeing the jaguar) and assessing (understanding where we stand with respect to the jaguar).

When my client Rosa came to me, she was emotionally numb; the only real feelings she could name were the ones related to her endometriosis, which caused her great physical pain. Her trauma, in her mind, was this health condition. Now, this doesn't mean that she was unaware of the suffering she'd experienced in her early years; however, she had no awareness that the trauma she'd experienced at a young age had influenced both her software and hardware. Rosa wore her "scars" with pride because she had to become a fighter in order to navigate a system that would just as soon see her fall into the cracks of society. She seldom talked about her past, except to say, "I made it through, so I'm living proof that anyone can do it."

However, this was a false badge of courage because she'd never stopped to consider the toll her trauma had taken on her, nor did she recognize how it had influenced the way she walked through life with a mask of resilience that hid the deeper pain and insecurities. When Rosa and I explored the depths of her ungrieved loss—of a "normal" childhood with functional parents, of a family that could love and honor the woman she'd become today—she was not so frightened of turning to face the jaguar. She was able to tell her life story from a place of empowerment, and to take responsibility for her present well-being.

At first, Rosa was reluctant to do this. It's also true that many people in therapeutic fields would suggest that such work is wild and triggering, but the only way to face the jaguar is head-on. Moreover, Rosa and I took time to build a strong rapport, and she had a long list of inner and outer resources to do the work of facing her jaguar.

She had been trained to believe that being a victim of the system makes us weak and powerless, and she didn't like feeling weak and powerless. Possibly, beloved friend, you understand her sentiments. I explained to Rosa that the first step to emerging from victimhood is *knowing* that we have been harmed; this is how we can take steps to validate and get clear about our experience, learn from it, and use it to uncover our grace and enrich our community. Rosa had been conditioned to "get over it" by uncaring adults who had no capacity to be with her suffering; in a way, she'd internalized this "get over it" mentality. However, when people think they do not have a right to experience the full spectrum of their feelings, they cut themselves off from munay, which makes awakening from suffering difficult.

Rosa also shared that, beneath her tough exterior, she was afraid of the idea of facing her jaguar. The possibility made her tremble, and looking at the entirety of her suffering made her feel she didn't have the strength. *You stupid girl, you want to face that predator? You don't stand a chance!* her internal dialogue retorted. We investigated that fear over time, and Rosa learned that it didn't have to be a battle in which she would either win or lose. The jaguar was not something outside herself that she had to fight; it was something inside her that she had to make peace with, simply by acknowledging its presence. This was the *knowing* part of her journey.

Then, we got into *assessing* her experience and beginning to draw the line between her physical pain and the emotional pain she'd been carrying for so long. How had she come to have such a split consciousness—where one part of her beamed its radiance out into the world, but the other part carried deep shame and brokenness? Through our work together, we came to understand that this was connected not just to her experience in the foster-care system, due to her parents' neglect, but it was also intergenerational. Both of her parents had been estranged from their families of origin. So, not only did her parents have to deal with the trauma of physical distance from everyone they'd ever known, but also the emotional distance that grew over time. The stitches in the manta had come undone, and both of Rosa's parents had learned to numb their pain with alcohol and other distractions. Rosa told me, "It was like I was living with carcasses—their spirits were long gone." They were incapable of attending to her needs. By the age of seven, Rosa was in and out of foster care; by the age of ten, it was her life.

The key to her journey toward reconciliation was when Rosa understood that her trauma hadn't just come from her individual choices or circumstances, but from a pattern that had also afflicted her parents and impacted their capacity to be there for her. She also came to accept that she'd disassociated from the hurtful circumstances of her environment; from an early age, she resolved never to cry or feel much of anything. "It was like being in jail," she recalls. "At first, numbing the feelings and pain about not having any of my family around was a defensive mechanism, because I didn't want the other people around me to sniff out my weakness and take advantage of it. Then, it became my way of life."

During our work together, Rosa recognized that this defense mechanism had served her well. Disassociation is an understandable choice, and sometimes, the only one we have. But over time, Rosa closed up even more tightly. Like many who find themselves in similar situations, she learned to carry her burdens on her back and closed her heart, which desensitized her to her own emotions. For her, this was a practical matter. Before she came to me, she didn't think she had the luxury to feel or to look back on her past.

But her assessment didn't stop there. Not only did she develop an awareness of where her trauma had come from, she also came to appreciate its unexpected gifts. She then went into the process of *reconciling* her wounds and *engendering* new forms of healing—the final two parts of KARE, which we'll discuss in the next chapters.

You may relate deeply to Rosa. Perhaps you've been in emotional, mental, and physical pain for as long as you can remember. Maybe you didn't always let yourself feel it. And maybe, when you did, pain offered its own refuge and inspiration.

Some of my pieces of writing were impregnated, labored, and birthed out of pain. I didn't necessarily know this until I started reading over them. I learned that woven into my pain is a deep sense of motivation. This isn't just about being a survivor. I also try to create environments for other people where they can show up as themselves. Growing up fast and early gave me a sense of perspective and playfulness that makes it easier for others to trust me and to express their authenticity. I was overjoyed to see that Rosa was beginning to open up, which also helped her understand her physical pain and cultivate a deeper trust in herself and her resilient sentipensante. Now, it was time for Rosa to recognize that she didn't have to keep fighting and enduring battles in order to be whole.

Ideally, the process of KARE is something that we get to experience in the presence of a warm, resonant companion or a nurturing support system. But many of us are not properly educated when it comes to acknowledging other people's feelings. By this, I'm not talking about a formal education to be a therapist, but simply the fact that our own pain can make it hard for us to listen to and accompany others in a similar state. In fact, due to our wounding, someone else's feelings might bring up discomfort within us, causing us to turn away. The result is a wound that we bear both individually and collectively: navigating life with a persistent sense of isolation.

KARE guides us to validate our own and other people's feelings and life experiences, and it enables us to build resilience and face life's inevitable challenges, including the ones associated with our post-trauma healing. We may long to be seen, heard, and acknowledged by others, but it really begins with practicing "self-breeding," in which we nurture ourselves by recognizing and accepting our sentipensante. We treat ourselves as whole beings, not continuing to fragment ourselves like a mechanical device with a series of disconnected functions.

While a lack of validation from those in our environment is always going to be painful, the way we show up and communicate with others has ripple effects. Beloved friend, you too can learn to offer yourself compassionate accompaniment and extend it to those whose capacity to show up for you is limited for reasons you may not be able to see or understand. Ultimately, the ways others in your circle show you consideration and validation are out of your control. What is in reach is the way you respond to hurtful situations, and whether you take responsibility as an active agent authoring the stories of your life. This is how you tap into the deep intelligence of the heart—the elixir of munay.

EMBODY THE JAGUAR

Connecting with Your Wound (KARE Method: Know and Assess)

This exercise addresses the *knowing* and *assessing* parts of the KARE method.

- When you don't feel safe enough to be with your emotional, physical, mental, and spiritual pain, what are the inner and outer resources you can call upon? Inner resources might be qualities you've already cultivated, such as self-compassion. Outer resources might be activities, such as dancing; people, such as a therapist or confidant; or places, such as the lake by your house, or other manifestations of Nature that you feel connected to that shore up your sense of inner safety and wholeness. Take some time to list your inner and outer resources in your journal.

- Know your wound. Similar to the majestic animals of the wild, you are being given a chance to validate your experiences and to accept the dimensions of your sentipensante. Where in your body are you feeling the wound? You may wish to intuitively draw the shape of the wound or give it colors that correspond to how it feels.

- Assess your wound: What are you feeling/thinking right now? I encourage you, beloved friend, to expand and explore the range of your feelings to become more precise about what you are feeling, beyond just sad, angry, hopeful, or fearful. Look for synonyms that can detail how you are feeling. Acknowledge this to yourself with unapologetic truth and radical intimacy. With each feeling or thought, write down where you think it comes from. For example: "I am feeling devastated. This is connected to the news I received this morning about a major health issue I'm having, but it also goes back to some of my experiences of being a sick child and teenager, and feeling my life was over before it began." Assessing the state of your sentipensante will help you to weigh the impact your wounding has had and continues to have on you.

4

TENDING THE FRAGMENTED SELF

Step "R" of KARE: Reconciliation

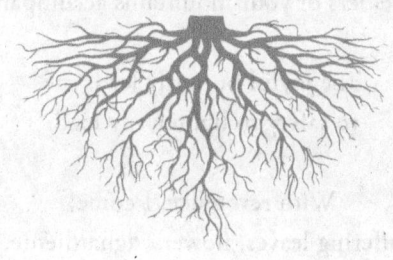

Pilgrimage

I walked up thousands of steps,
carrying heavy gifts in the tattered pockets of my soul,
collected along the way of my melancholy.

Beneath my feet, life moves under the twilight,
and with each step, I bow
to those rejoicing in the darkness.

Your flowered veil plays with my naked heart,
and in the desolation among your trees,
I hear the elders of your mountains accompanying me.

The joyful butterfly leads me
to safety to lighten my load.

With reverence, I come,
offering leaves, flowers, aguardiente,
and tobacco to the wrinkled abuelas
sitting at the threshold of life.

Longing to nest near their lips, I am
to listen to their stories carried by the winds.

Despair dimmed my footprints
when I faced the silence of falling trees,
and the depths of my neglected grief.

I shook, screamed, and greeted fear,
until the wind, transmuted into melodies,
woke me from the nightmare in daylight.

Your roots revealed themselves,
and I knew I stood on sacred ground.

I blew my winds into the leaves,
poured aguardiente, spread tobacco,
called the one who makes me holy,
and let my weary skin be the feast.

My walk downhill is lighter now.
My steps are engraved on your flowery veil.

Beloved, rejoice with me!
My renewed and reunited soul
is coming back home with me.

When I became intimate with my wounding, I learned to validate the parts of me that were waiting for my attention. My search took me through long retreats in which I learned about how to restore the body, as well as the philosophical frameworks that connect the symptoms of the physical body and the afflictions of the mind. I was beginning to learn how to inhabit my body, but this wasn't an easy process. Often, I couldn't interiorize the information being delivered. Being asked to deeply feel my body didn't seem accessible, as none of it felt safe to me.

I didn't know it at the time, but so many of the protocols that are established to support people in facing and processing their wounding are not always effective because they fail to take into account the cultural context and/or information about how and where the trauma originated. Instead, they assume a unilateral prescription that will work for everyone, regardless of their circumstances. It's little wonder that I couldn't relate to the ways trauma and stress were presented to me. Although Quechua is not my first language, Peruvian culture in general is influenced by Quechua and Andean thought. For one thing, there is no mental concept of *trauma* in Quechua; instead, there is more of an embodied understanding of a person's sentipensante after the traumatic event.

Beloved friend, it's possible that you've also been in search of the source of your own disconnection—the ripped threads of your manta. Perhaps the prescriptive methods that you have discovered have felt limited and incomplete. My hope is that this chapter will nourish you by guiding you into the R of KARE: *reconciliation*. Reconciliation is a process of deep reunion with the part of you that has been splintered by your wounding. Reconciliation is not merely a mental journey; it is a visceral process of calling your nuna back.

Although the concept of nuna is a large umbrella under which many different aspects of the larger self are contained, it can be thought of as the soul. In Spanish, the word *animu* or *anima* can be translated as "soul" or "spirit" and is often used interchangeably with nuna in Andean therapeutic settings. However, the meaning of nuna is untranslatable in Quechua, as it goes beyond our linguistic comprehension. It is a very expansive word that speaks to both our divine and earthly origins. It doesn't have a clear connotation because it doesn't fit into linear or Judeo-Christian ideas about the soul.

Nuna is an expression of the multiverse and Nature together. It's also our consciousness—the thing that makes us human, gives us autonomy, and moves us. Nuna can also be metaphorically referred to as the *shadow*, the part of a person's essence that's capable of leaving the physical body when wounding occurs; however, even this concept of the shadow is a simplification. I'm not referring to the shadow in the classic Jungian way, where we may have repressed or shoved parts of ourselves into the unconscious mind, nor am I referring to it in the literal sense. Nuna is the aspect of our existence that's the convergence point between the seen and unseen realms, as well as the dimensions of will, memory, and consciousness. The seen realm is that of earth and matter, whereas the unseen realm is the mysterious region in which the void and the infinite multiverse exist. Nuna is meant to exist in both.

Nuna includes three aspects, according to Pacha philosophy: *samay* (breath), *supay* (energy), and *nuna* itself (power or autonomy). In general terms, nuna is the animating force we are given from the time we are incubated in our mother's womb and beyond. It is the place where our memories, feelings, and emotions reside. Nuna is like the dust of the stars, or the water that makes the sea, but it is not the same as any of these. It is connected to the elements, but because it transcends comprehension, our encounters with nuna can never be bound by concepts or language. All the metaphors we use to talk about nuna are only ways to approximate its true meaning.

We cannot address our suffering without recognizing the role of nuna—and reconciling with it. Nuna and the physical body are inextricable, in the same way we experience simultaneity of thought and feeling in a state of sentipensante. Although nuna and the body can appear to be separate, especially in experiences of wounding, they are not independent, and intentional embodiment allows us to experience reintegration.

While chapter 5 will go into greater detail about how we can make the body and external environment safe places to come back to, we must first recognize the circumstances that may have caused our nuna to split—otherwise the attempt to be in our bodies will not be sustainable. After all, there is a reason we feel disconnected, and that reason has to do with the sense of danger that ruptured our autonomy and the connection between the body and nuna. We may not be able to identify all of these moments of rupture, as many experiences of wounding are preverbal and don't come with tangible memories, or the impact of the event is so shocking that memories get buried. However, it's possible to bring our nuna closer to us.

Nuna is a primordial language and consciousness of Pacha. It is the force that longs for order and harmony—and it is our task to recognize how near or far it is from us, as well as how far we are from the natural world and a sense of community. In this chapter, you'll gain a deeper understanding of circumstances that may have resulted in an unbalanced energy—which also creates a dismemberment from infinite creation, almost as if we are a loose thread in the manta of life. Nature plays an important role here, as it is often embedded in the places where we experienced fragmentation from nuna. By beginning to work with Nature as the source from which we come and an ally to whom we pay the greatest respect, we can draw the aspect of our nuna that has left even closer. In Quechua, this is known as *waqyaykuy*, the act of calling back our nuna and restoring the self to wholeness.

I do not want to romanticize this process, as it is a profound one with many layers, some of which can be difficult to work through. However, it is possible to cultivate tools that enable us to understand where we may have left our nuna, and to gather the medicines that can help us collect it—or at least ensure that it's safeguarded until we have the resources to bring it home.

There is a Spanish saying, *Mi alma está rota en mil pedazos*, which translates to, "My soul is broken into a thousand pieces." If you have ever felt this way, please remember that this is a normal part of our complex human experience. But you are not meant to languish in a state of disconnection from your true grace and sacred manta. You are meant to reconcile with your nuna.

UNDERSTANDING SUSTO AND NUNA

You have come to *know* and *assess* your wounding—the first two parts of the KARE method. From here, you enter the process of *reconciliation*, which is about reconnecting with your nuna and bringing it home to your body.

You are now also beginning to understand the sentipensante associated with your wounding, as well as the memories and circumstances surrounding it. But please know that because we're not just a mind separated from a body and vice versa, the process of coming into wholeness is gradual. It doesn't happen all at once. We've been habituated to think more than we feel, but we aren't a machine that can be separated into different functions. We are visceral. As you work with the processes in this book, you'll gradually build the bridge between thinking and feeling, and it will become more natural to you.

Although it is never our fault that we were harmed, we can better understand the source of our fear and wounding, and our responsibility as a parent, a friend, a community member, etc. This is how we develop the agency to restore our wholeness.

In common parlance, according to neurobiology, we experience trauma when we perceive a situation as threatening or dangerous, and when our autonomy is lost or taken from us—but we are not able to complete a fight-or-flight response. In a sense, we don't "bounce back" to a state of equilibrium. The trauma gets "stuck" in our body, meaning it is lodged inside us and keeps us in a state of physical and psychological immobility. Freezing is a common reaction to trauma or fear. We may also experience disassociation, a survival reflex that disconnects us from our body or puts us into a spiritless "carcass" mode. It's important to note that not everyone who experiences a traumatic event experiences trauma. Everyone has their own stress threshold. Trauma occurs when that threshold is crossed and we feel unable to cope with the situation at hand.

It's as if our software, or inner coding, gets programmed with trauma's message, causing our hardware, or our body and physical manifestation, to cease to function in the way it's meant to. We can no longer feel a sense of grace, and as time passes, it's as if we're doomed to relive our most challenging moments, which may rise to the surface—in our sentipensante—when we perceive a threat, whether real or imagined.

Many Western modes of trauma care use their own frameworks for looking at this. For example, a trauma professional might suggest that the nervous system collapsed after a traumatic incident. Rooted in Pacha philosophy, I see it in a different way. As a result of trauma, our nuna flees our body, leading to a sense of disconnection and imbalance. This is the result of *susto*, Spanish for "fright," or a state of shock that can make us feel separate from our body—because some part of our animating force and psyche has, in fact, fled from us.

Nuna is energy that can freely enter and exit the body. Nuna also has its own set of memories. It cannot be destroyed, but when it is absent, it literally struggles to animate the body. When we have the felt sense of "animation," of understanding that we and all beings (including non-humans) are "ensouled," we naturally have greater compassion toward one another. However, there are many "walking dead"—those who are like spiritless carcasses, with little to no empathy for themselves or others. In Pacha philosophy, we can understand this absence of empathy toward humans, animals, and other life forms as a disconnection from nuna.

Although nuna does not live exclusively in the body, an animated body that loses part of its nuna is bound to break the balance of wellness.

The mind loses control, sometimes leading to unconsciousness. Memory becomes unclear, and strength decreases. Doesn't this sound similar to the modern affliction of anxiety? Anxiety is often associated with the loss of autonomy after a traumatic event. This anxiety can get transmuted into post-traumatic stress disorder (PTSD), the diminishing of a personal sense of self, and the inability to process our experiences.

After we enter a state of susto, the body can suffer from ailments that a Nuna Kamayuq will recognize with the assistance of Nature. For example, perhaps you experience prolonged sickness, depression, loss of appetite, or debilitating pain that has no explanation. You might be visited by vivid or disturbing dreams, or you might be jumpy during slumber—which is an indication that part of your nuna is roaming and battling the forces of another realm. You might lose a sense of mental clarity. You might suffer from excessive perspiration or an accelerated heartbeat. It is similar to being a body suit of flesh and organs—but without animation, because a part of your nuna has left you. You may walk around in such a state for years without realizing it, until things reach a fever pitch and you are desperately in search of harmony. In fact, this is true for many who've been dealing with the repercussions of their susto for years, perhaps decades. Sometimes, we are too numb or habituated to our circumstances to realize it, until our symptoms are undeniable.

There's a common saying in Perú: *Perdió la cabeza*, or "He/she has lost their head." Essentially, this means someone has lost the capacity to think or reason, and they are disconnected from reality. When taken to extremes, this can result in some kind of breakdown, but it can also take the form of susceptibility to false mental constructs, such as low self-worth and other stories we tell ourselves. The head gives us the capacity to collect, understand, and produce knowledge about ourselves; it also helps us make sense of our relationship with Nature, the conditions of our lives, and our responsibilities as individuals in a larger community.

When we have a healthy relationship with our nuna, we are in harmony. However, when contrary external activity generates susto and our nuna splits, this impacts our cognition, thinking processes, and ultimately, our autonomy—causing us to collapse under the weight of our wounding.

HOW FAR IS YOUR NUNA?

Before I go any further, I want to clarify what I mean when I talk about nuna leaving us. It is not so much that our nuna is "stuck" in a particular place or geographic location outside of us. We are multidimensional beings who exist in a state beyond time or place. Pacha philosophy invites us to realize that everything around us is alive and multidimensional; therefore, everything holds its own animating force, which is in constant exchange with our nuna. Indeed, we are in constant connection with Nature, people, material things, and thoughtforms, so when we experience susto, we become linked with all of these. Our nuna is now a part of them.

On some level, all of us experience a degree of disconnection from our nuna. We live fragmented, as fragmentation is a consequence of our human makeup. This is not "bad" in and of itself, as it awakens our sense of agency and awareness that we're embedded in all the things we encounter. But it is when our nuna is "far" from us—meaning it has significantly detached from us and become overly enmeshed with other beings—that our experience of susto becomes debilitating.

The degree to which our nuna has become enmeshed with other beings is dependent on the nature of our susto. We can experience susto for many reasons, ranging from abuse at the hands of another, to injuries, accidents, illness, surgery, and natural events. Intergenerational trauma can also create susto, and a lot of this has to do with the fear that is passed down to us by our caregivers.

Finally, going into Nature with the assumption that we're above it, having a false hierarchical attitude that infuses many of our cultures and societies, and treating it without the proper respect or precautions can result in susto. This is why we must approach Nature as the living entity it is, with reverence. We may have a lot of romantic ideas about Nature, but it has both heavy and light aspects. Nature, as our primal ancestor and source of life, has the power to devour, destroy, and even abort us. We must learn to discern when we are approaching Nature with arrogance or the need to dominate, even if these attitudes lie beneath the surface. It is best to ask for permission and to "feel into" whether Nature is receiving us well. After all, Nature has been neglected and abused, and like any living entity, it is hungry and eager for intimacy. Thus, our nuna can be the perfect meal to satisfy its needs.

Under most circumstances, it is possible to get a sense of when our nuna has separated and fled from us. We lose our sense of aliveness and reality, and our behavior changes. We can sense that something is off. We might be haunted by memories, or we walk around feeling a lack of integration with our core essence. We might look for answers from conventional medicine by visiting doctors who insist that all is well, even though we know that's not true—because the body talks, especially when its nuna is far. It can talk to us through any number of uncomfortable experiences that permeate our sentipensante: feelings of detachment, emptiness, lack of purpose and motivation, aimlessness, depression, and profound sadness. Simply moving can feel like a hard task to accomplish, which may translate to a pain that ripples into anger and resentment toward life.

Even when our nuna has fled, calling it back to us benefits our human experience. And, truth be told, our nuna is always calling to us, reminding us that it's our job to weave ourselves back into it.

I've heard teachers and elders ask, "Can you see your nuna? Can you play with it? How far is it from you?" In many ways, the ability to determine answers to these questions is a part of the A in KARE: assessment. However, in Western culture, the capacity to make such an assessment on our own is challenging, as we are not well-versed in the codes of nuna. This is why I hope for this chapter to offer a meaningful guide for reconciling with your nuna.

In retrospect, looking back on the time when I was in the midst of severe depression and anxiety, I could feel that my nuna was far from me. I knew my nuna was there, but I was busily occupied by distractions, so that I couldn't "play" with it and bring it back to me. Many of us tend to be in a state of constant warfare that keeps our attention occupied. Our responses to our natural environment, as well as political and socioeconomic concerns, can create a constant need to "defend" against the world, which takes up a lot of energy. These are the collective predicaments of our existence that can result in "sickness" or "illness" and that may expose us to susto and remove our attention from our nuna, which longs to return to us.

All of this is attended by consequences that are larger than our individual suffering. We all belong to larger communities—including villages, cities, ethnic groups, nations, religions, and so on. Each of these entities has its own nuna. We are a totality made of many interlocking parts. This is why we must remember that our individual healing is directly connected to our collective healing. In addition, the care of the human body (flesh, mind, and spirit) is complex and needs to be considered in the context of everything that may serve to destabilize it: cultural, spiritual, and geopolitical. When any of the pieces in the realm of our existence are "broken," all of us end up suffering. When anything in Nature is altered, our human bodies experience this, too. Thus, diagnosing the extent to which our nuna has become severed is integral to living well. It helps us understand not just our individual context, but our collective context, as well as how we are managing our resources and ecosystems.

In the Andean world, we have a number of specialists who are able to assist people, depending on the type of sickness they experience. Just as there are medical doctors in the Western world who specialize in treating different parts of the body and different illnesses, the "spiritual doctors" of the Andes address a number of complex maladies. They are vital members of their communities and offer their service by sharing their gifts and expressing their abilities. Their work is based on the meticulous observation and interpretation of phenomena in Nature and our human lives that we might take for granted, or that we fail to see clearly if we are rooted in a materialist observation of the universe that does not take into account the unseen realms. Thus, Andean doctors are the mediators, intercessors, custodians of knowledge, and weavers between realms. They embody wisdom and integrity, and interpret the codes of the unseen and infinite for the person who is seeking assistance. Accordingly, my own accepted "responsibility" these days is to serve as a guide who assists people—including you, beloved friend—to gain the awareness of how far away their nuna is, and to do the important work of calling it back.

TRUSTING AND RESPECTING NATURE

When I began working to heal my wounding, I realized how split I felt—physically, emotionally, and spiritually. I'd learned that, according to Western conventions of trauma healing, I "should" be in my body because that was good for me. However, I *wasn't* in my body.

During my reconciliation process, a series of memories came washing over me. This is another reason I highly recommend working with a skilled specialist—a teacher or counselor who can guide you through the painful moments. Some of my memories were extremely vivid and painful, and others not so much—but I understood they were all arising because it was my job to reconcile with them. As I was contemplating the moments in my life when I experienced susto and when my nuna left my body, the memory of nearly drowning as a small child came rushing back. It was a moment of complete terror that had been carved deeply into my perceptions, even though I seldom thought about it consciously. Young and innocent, I had swum out into the ocean, paying little heed to my abuelita's remonstrances that Nature is not to be messed with. I didn't realize I was courting trouble; I didn't realize the water was hungry and needed to eat . . . and there I was, offering myself as food.

The water was so hungry that it took two lifeguards to rescue me. In fact, as we got closer to shore, the water pulled me back out—twice. This memory was something that required assistance from my spiritual *maestro* (teacher), Amaru, who has guided me through many aspects of my own healing for many years now. Although it is possible to call our nuna back on our own—for example, if our nuna left due to an accident, a surgery, a trauma related to another person, or an unavoidable natural event—there are circumstances under which it is not advisable to do this. Please be cautious and work with a trusted spiritual teacher if you determine that your nuna fled from you due to neglect or lack of consideration toward the natural, living world and all its dimensions—for example, if you went into the natural world or sacred grounds without taking necessary precautions or honoring its primordial potency. This is not to blame you for your actions. Please note, beloved friend, that many of us are raised in cultures that either don't have or have lost spiritual protocols for working with Nature and encouraging a reciprocal relationship with the animate world. You should also work with a specialist if your susto is the result of plant medicine–induced altered states, which can change one's spiritual DNA.

My main point here is this: Nature is not to be trifled with! It is billions of years old, and our existence as humans is miniscule in comparison. We are still being cooked within Nature's cauldron, meaning that if our susto is the result of messing with that process in some way, however unintentional, we cannot expect to march into Nature and demand that our nuna be returned to us! We must remember our intentions do not always match the impact of our actions. We will need the support of a spiritual intercessor to bring our nuna back. Sometimes, this will require specially prepared physical interventions with plant, animal, and mineral medicine. This precise medicine should be provided by someone who knows how to deal with the potency of Nature in the multidimensional realms, otherwise it will create more harm and keep our nuna away from us. We will further discuss what it means to find a good teacher, and to exercise discernment and respect in working with elders and teachers, in chapter 8. For now, it's a good idea to pay attention to your gut and sentipensante if you are considering working with a teacher.

When I worked with my spiritual maestro, Amaru, to address my childhood trauma of nearly drowning, he informed me, "Part of your nuna is with the water that almost took you, and you have to bring it back." Amaru had done a consultation with the unseen realm using coca leaves, and he determined that a sacred contract was the best way to call my nuna back and to make peace with those waters. Until that point, I hadn't been back to the beach where I almost drowned, but I certainly felt the pull of those waters.

While the sacred contract brought a sense of balance and closure, I became aware that I may never be able to fully recover that piece of my nuna, at least in the way that my Western mindset might think of integration. However, I recovered the part of my nuna that needed to continue living, while knowing some part of me will always belong to those waters.

When I began doing the work of calling my nuna back, I came to a deeper appreciation of why I had so much reverence for the water. Water has brought me a sense of rejuvenation, healing, and connection to the seen and unseen parts of the multiverse. When I was a child, the ocean was hungry and took my nuna. Now, years later, in the aftermath of the reconciliation process I did with Amaru, I have wholeheartedly given part of my nuna to the waters and asked them to safeguard it. Now, the natural force of the waters that almost killed me has become my relative, my guardian, and the custodian of my secrets and strengths.

Amaru and I performed a sacred contract that called in the sweetest parts of the ocean, which carries all qualities: wild and ravenous, as well as nurturing and life-affirming. And although that part of my nuna is still there on that beach where it was stolen so many years ago, I fully trust that it is safe—and exactly where it needs to be.

CALLING OUR NUNA BACK

When we call back our nuna, we are calling back our animating force and claiming our right to recuperate, to inhabit ourselves so that we are one with our body-heart-spirit, and so we can be fully human. Bringing our nuna back after a susto is equivalent to reclaiming autonomy over our life. In chapter 5, we'll get into more ways to reclaim our autonomy in the long term, so that our nuna can come back to and sustain us with our life force.

We regularly receive wake-up calls from our nuna, who *wants* to come back to us. The oldest part of our nuna is connected to the eternal and is always giving us insight to balance what's out of order. We essentially have two choices: We can continue to carry on, sleepwalking, remaining in spiritless carcass mode so that our experience of our aliveness is limited. Or, we can voluntarily call our nuna back to us. A lot of times, we can do so in a simple and loving way. For example, if you had a nickname that your family called you when you were young, you might offer positive reinforcement to your nuna by lovingly using that nickname as you call out to it. The sooner you call your nuna back, the better, but your body has to be ready, like a sacred vessel, to receive it. In these moments, your focus must be on making the body livable and capable of being reanimated.

You might sense that your body does not yet feel safe or that there is further work you need to do on the K and A parts of KARE (knowing and assessing your wounds.) There is no need to rush this process. In fact, rushing the process can worsen matters. This is extremely important if you are going through a period of tremendous change, such as divorce, job loss, the death of a loved one, moving out of your home, or any kind of major disruption or shake-up. Even if the body isn't ready, you can still focus on making the body sacred ground to be inhabited by your nuna. In addition, you can acknowledge that your nuna is in the spirit realm and ask protectors, such as ancestral spirits or a manifestation of Nature that you feel close to, to offer comfort to your nuna as it wanders. In fact, in cases where you did not directly experience a trauma that was connected to tempting Nature, you can ask it to safeguard your nuna while you work to make your body a safe place to come back to.

If calling your nuna back feels daunting, you can work with someone to accompany you in this process. This is the kind of work that I routinely do with my clients. We spend a great deal of time on the K and A parts of the KARE process before we move into the R of reconciliation.

One of my clients, Isabella, was struggling with strong sensations from a preverbal memory as she contemplated the wounding she'd experienced in her lifetime. She told me that she had a feeling something terrible had happened when she was a toddler, and that the susto of the experience had caused her nuna to flee. She didn't have a clear memory of what had happened. I told her, "You don't have to know all the circumstances around your susto in order to bring your nuna closer. All you have to know is that it is far from you and you're ready to call it back."

Isabella understood that she was not yet ready to bring her nuna all the way home, but I suggested that she ask one of her outdoor plants to safeguard her nuna for a while until she was ready to welcome it home.

Isabella, who called her nuna Bella, said, "Bella, I know you're close to me. Please rest and animate this plant until my body is prepared to fully integrate with your animating force."

I helped Isabella to select the plant to safeguard her nuna, because her mind needed something tangible she could touch in order to remember that her nuna was close by and could be called back when she was ready. With my guidance, we created a sacred contract for this experience.

Please note that if you are not familiar with making sacred contracts, it's a good idea to work with a teacher who can guide you through the process. Taking your time to do this work with the utmost respect and reverence is important. You might know if you've overlooked the codes for a sacred contract because Pacha will always have ways to tell you. This could come through a vivid dream or symbolic situations in your life. For example, I have conducted incomplete sacred contracts, only to notice that my plants' leaves become twisted and distorted shortly thereafter; this helped me to understand that my process itself was twisted and distorted.

Please don't let this be a cause for apprehension, but an opportunity to pay your respects to the unseen realms. A sacred contract does not have to be elaborate, but it *does* need to be attended to with sincerity and care. I'll walk you through an example in the Embody the Jaguar exercise at the end of this chapter. Be sure to seek guidance if you are uncertain about sacred contracts. And most of all, know that being in a reciprocal relationship with Nature can go a long way. Nature is inherently powerful and resilient, and it can safeguard our fragmented parts until we are ready to reclaim them. As I assured Isabella, there is no shame if you don't feel resourced enough to reclaim the parts of your nuna that have fractured off from you.

Reclamation of our nuna is an ongoing process, and the more you prioritize it, the easier it will become to bring it closer. You will know when it's time to start bringing your nuna back to your body when inhabiting your body actually starts feeling more pleasurable. At that point, you'll have the necessary resources to bring your nuna home.

MIRROR THE JAGUAR

Mapping Your Experiences of Susto (KARE Method: Reconcile)

A *paqarina* is a Quechua term that describes the place of origin of a person, as well as the creation center of ancestors considered sacred beings. A paqarina generally corresponds to natural formations connected to the place where you were born. As we move around, we make conscious and unconscious connections with other sacred places in Nature. You can always reconnect with the paqarina of your birthplace, which protects your path in the world.

This exercise encompasses the *reconciliation* part of the KARE method.

- Consider where you were born. What are the natural manifestations—mountains, seas, forests, etc.—of your paqarina?

- Your answers to the first question may give you a sense of how to work with the elements. But so will the traditions of your family. What are the traditions—special foods and beverages, festivals, celebrations, etc.—that made a mark on your life at a young age?

- What was your family of origin like when you were growing up? How did your caregivers behave toward you, and you toward them?

- Did you feel safe and accepted growing up? What did you have to do to experience a sense of safety?

- Who in your life was there to offer you comfort?

- At what point did you leave home? Who were you in these new places?

- Based on your responses to all of the above, consider your experiences of susto. Refer back to the list of your wounding experiences that you created in chapter 3. Is your

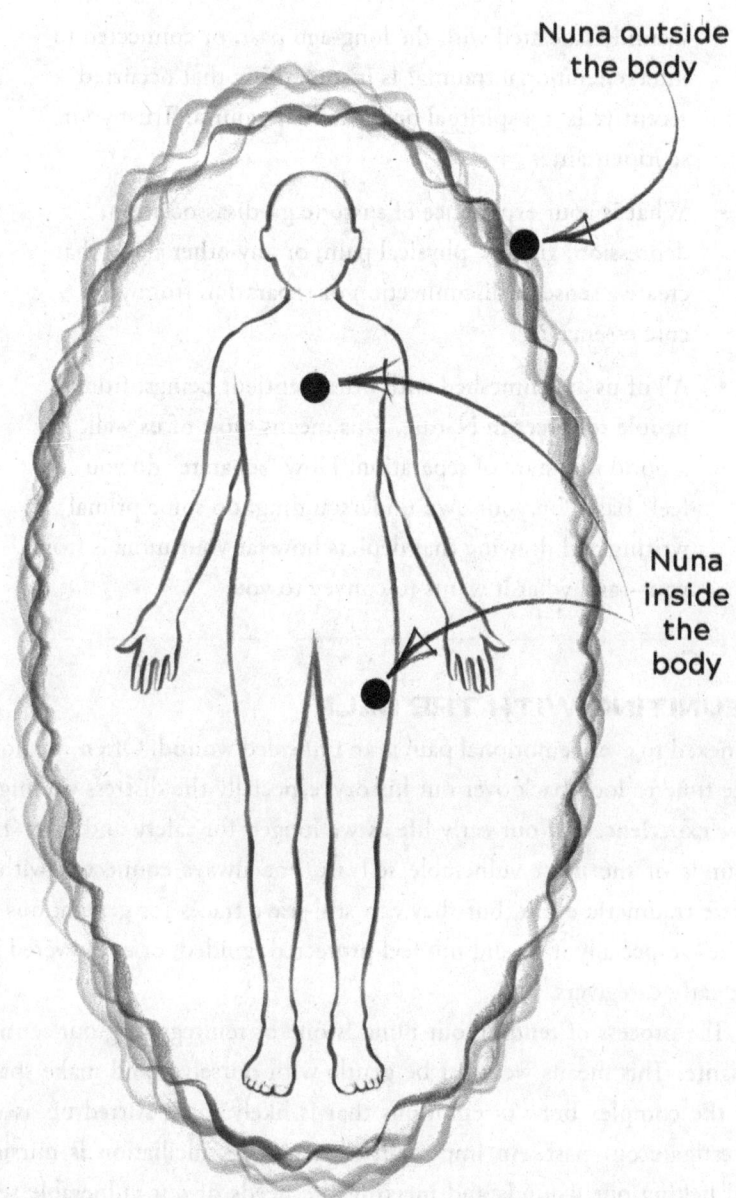

Nuna, our animated energy, moves between the body and the space around it. When detached, it disrupts balance and may cause susto. This graphic encourages reflection: Is your nuna within the area of pain or wandering outside? Identifying its location is key to restoring wellness and harmony.

wound associated with the long-ago past, or connected to intergenerational trauma? Is it something that occurred recently? Is it a spiritual or existential wound? Trust your sentipensante.

- What is your experience of susto (e.g., disassociation, depression, anxiety, physical pain, or any other states that create a sense of disconnection or separation from your core essence)?

- All of us are enmeshed with other sentient beings, from people to forces in Nature. This means most of us walk around in a state of separation. How "separate" do you feel? Based on your own understanding, do some primal writing and drawing that depicts how far your nuna is from you—and what it wants to convey to you.

REUNITING WITH THE SELF

Annexed to every emotional pain is an unhealed wound. Often, we don't take time to look back over our history, especially the distress we might have experienced in our early life as we longed for safety and love. The wounds of the most vulnerable self are not always connected with a severe traumatic event, but they can still leave traces for generations to come—especially if we did not feel protected, guided, or empowered by our early caregivers.

The process of tending our nuna is one of reintegrating our sentipensante. This means we must be gentle with ourselves and make space for the complex brew of emotions that is likely to be stirred up as we investigate our past. An important aspect of reconciliation is nursing and licking our wounds and meeting the needs of our vulnerable self. When we are not aware of its tender essence, we may become reactive and experience outbursts of emotion, which can leave us depleted by shame and frustration. Additionally, everyone in our circle can suffer when this happens.

If you feel that reconciliation with your vulnerable self is necessary, you can softly speak to it: "Beloved vulnerable self, it's me. Please forgive me. I didn't pay enough attention to you, and I dismissed your pain for years. You are safe now. I am here for you." By bearing witness to your vulnerable self, you are weaving a sustainable root system for impactful healing.

Calling our nuna home is a process of reconciling with our underlying suffering and offering consolation and comfort to our vulnerable self, who is usually in exile because of the ways we've learned to distract ourselves. When we draw the fragments of who we are closer together, we experience a joyful reunion. This sweet reconciliation of all the fragmented parts is similar to a wave touching the shore before it finds its way back to the vast ocean of being of which it was always a part.

We must be courageous in order to live under the all-seeing eye of Pacha, which gives but also takes. When I speak to clients who tell me that they're not confident enough to do this work, I playfully yet sincerely say, "Open your hand. Here's your courage. Please take it. I'm giving it back to you." It took courage for us to come into this earthly plane, and although we may feel like we lost that courage somewhere along the way, we can always take it back. We can always choose to embody the jaguar!

Recovering the essence of our nuna is tantamount to taking actions that bring us closer to living full and complete lives—walking in Nature, tending our gardens, supporting our community. We can also work with preventative protocols in our modern lives, which helps us increase our resources for tapping into courage. This process of reuniting with the seed of who we are and self-breeding the vulnerable self, whose primordial tenderness longs for reconnection, is a process of walking more intentionally with and toward our own medicine. Often, the medicine that will restore harmony at our roots is much closer to home than we may think it is. The process of digging into our roots and understanding our wounds can bring us closer and closer to our true medicine(s)—which may include ancestral foods, physical movement, or anything else that increases our sense of fully belonging to Nature.

This process of reunion allows us to become integrated members of Pacha who are capable of moving through all the dimensions of our lives from a stable center. As you experience harmony and unification, you will tap into your own sweetness so deeply that you will be able to accept all parts of who you are, including the so-called "darkness" and "wounding" that you may have struggled with for so long.

EMBODY THE JAGUAR

A Pilgrimage for Your Nuna (KARE Method: Reconcile)

This process can occur after you've made contact with your nuna; it will entail asking a place in Nature to safeguard your nuna until you are ready to do the work of reconciling your body with it. Here, I am placing the jaguar squarely in front of you, so that you can experience the rawness of your sentipensante. I encourage you to rely on the internal and external resources that you noted in chapter 3, and to do this process when you are ready.

This exercise encompasses the *reconciliation* part of the KARE method.

- Take a pilgrimage to a sacred place in Nature where you will imagine yourself coming face-to-face with and picking up the pieces of your nuna that are far from you.

- The place in Nature does not have to be somewhere remote or "grand," like the Himalayas or Machu Picchu. It might simply be a hiking trail at a local park.

- As you enter this space, ask Nature for permission to be here. Find the place where you'd like to sit for your sacred contract. Offer gratitude and care for the land in whatever way feels right.

- Recognize the range of painful emotions and situations in your life, especially the ones you have tended to relive over and over again. There may be an experience that feels especially challenging that you want to acknowledge here. This may feel convoluted, but for this process, you are going to offer your experiences to Nature as food. You will feel yourself peeling these layers off and saying to Nature, "I am giving you my fear toward this situation, my anger toward these people, my physical pain and terror around sickness, my disappointment in myself. I give you all that is heavy, and with reverence, I bring you this delicious meal, asking that you take it from me and eat it. Thank you."

- Now that you've offered what is heavy, and you've opened the mouth of Pacha, take a moment to make your petition to Nature. There might be a specific tree, plant, or area in this place that you want to appeal to directly. With great respect, ask Nature to safeguard the part of your nuna that is fragmented until the time is right to do the full reconciliation process of bringing it home to your body. You might say, "Although I don't know where my misplaced nuna went, I am asking if you can please safeguard it until I am ready to bring it home to myself."

- Listen for Pacha, and do not proceed until you feel you have received a yes and that your "food" offering has been accepted. You will also want to determine if you've received a no, and a message behind the no. Perhaps it's not the right time or the right element in Nature (e.g., water, plant, tree, mountain) to which to entrust your nuna. Consider going somewhere else instead—perhaps a place that carries the primal essence of the element to which you feel most connected.

- Close your sacred contract with intention, being sure to clean up after yourself and avoid breaking the natural balance that could end up doing harm. Once again, thank Nature for holding your nuna for you.

Now, there is a contract between you and Nature. From here on out, you can make mini-pilgrimages to this place and talk to your misplaced nuna. You can acknowledge that you've asked Nature to safeguard it. You might speak affectionately to it, sing songs to it, and simply let it know that you are here, and that it is safe in the meantime. You can also assure it that you will be reunited when the time is right.

Eventually, you will recognize when you are ready for "reassembly." At this point, you can go back to this place and begin to call your nuna home. You might say, "Little one, I'm asking you to come closer, so that we can be reunited." Also be sure to thank Nature once more for its willingness to keep this misplaced nuna safe and secure.

I encourage you to give this process time and not to rush anything, as most people won't be immediately ready to call their nuna back. The practices in chapter 5 will help you to make your body a safe space, so that your nuna can be welcomed home in due time.

5

MAKING THE BODY A SAFE PLACE TO COME HOME TO

Step "E" of KARE: Engendering Healing in Long-Lasting Ways

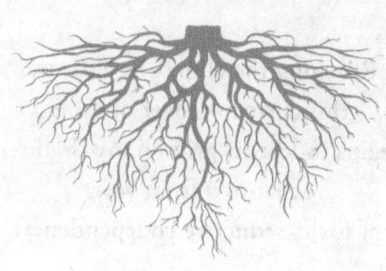

Making Love to My Fears

I make love to my fears
in the sensual moments,
remembering the warmth and power
my womb holds.

Loving my fears in bed,
in the shower,
and in moments of radical intimacy.

My body feels it all,
my breath caught
in its subtle, lingering touch.

Reaching the climax of pleasure,
this corrosive lover of mine
begins to lose its grip on my thighs—
exhausted from years
of toxic, seductive codependency.

Finally, I enjoy making love to you,
oh, fears of mine.

Reclaiming my body,
feeling my skin,
I love you in my womb.

I feel you deeply,
I scream pleasure silence pain,
nauseated as you search for the deepest
unseen darkness in me.

I make love to my fears
like never before,
reaching the height,
drenched in sweat from the sensory connection.

I whisper between sobs,
"I feel you!
I feel you!
I feel you, fears of mine—and it is done!"

In the dark of my sacred womb,
I transmute you
into divine power.

Lying down, I remember how you once hurt,
how you paralyzed me—
now I see you, inebriated with pleasure,
holding onto my legs
as I say, "Goodbye, lover of mine."

The first time I heard the phrase, "The issues are in your tissues," I was in a yoga teacher training. I got into a pose with my belly against the floor and my upper body supported by the strength of my arms. As I moved softly from side to side, I took in the calming voice and presence of my teacher.

"Imagine you are letting go of the physical tension and discomfort from your chest and heart," she whispered. "Remember, we carry more than muscles and tissues inside our skin. Our issues are in our tissues."

A flash of insight pulsed through me. My heart felt unburdened as I continued to gently move my shoulders and head. Tears coursed down my face. Surprisingly, I wasn't self-conscious about the fact that others would see me crying. I just wanted time to stop. In this place where all my worries seemed somehow smaller, I had touched a moment of freedom that I wanted to freeze for eternity. The happiness inside my chest was bubbly and full, as well as unfamiliar. As I breathed out, I felt like I was finally in my body, and it was one of the most intimate experiences of my life. I felt safe in my body: safe enough to feel it all, see it all, taste it all, hear it all, touch it all. I was present, completely *here*. It felt like my senses were making love to me in the most tender way possible, gently welcoming me back home to myself.

It all begins and ends with the body. The body is the portal to our most exalted and unbearable experiences. It is the link between celestial and terrestrial, between the upper world and the underworld. Our human experiences—including the good ones, the not-so-good ones, and the ones with varied flavors in between—are captured and imprinted in our physical bodies, which are containers of history. While the body has the capacity to keep us close to reality and to act as the interface between our inner and outer world, it also holds traces of our hardships. This is why so many of us, including myself, have found it extremely difficult to relax the body and to simply abide with the factual reality that's unfolding.

However, when we look closer, the body reveals everything we're attempting to push away or keep from feeling. But we cannot truly push any of it away because our issues literally live inside our tissues, which yearn for sweetness and acknowledgment. Redirecting our gentle attention to the body requires the willingness to witness reality as it is.

Sometimes, shedding our layers won't feel accessible or safe for all of us, which is why I believe we must each intuit when it's the right time to begin the inner exploration of germinating the deep wisdom of the body. It begins with acknowledging that we have a body. This body tells a powerful story about our life experiences and our potential. It is both the path and the destination.

As you are reading this chapter, I invite you to situate yourself. Where are you? Where is your body? Are you aware—I mean, *really* aware—that you have a body? Do you know what it is communicating to you in this moment? Are you far from your body? Are you close to it? Is it easy or difficult to feel and sense? Do you tend to numb yourself so that it is challenging to recognize the signals your body is sending you?

Throughout this chapter, we will delve into not just the importance of inhabiting our bodies and learning gentle methods of welcoming ourselves home, but also of taking back our autonomy. We leave our bodies because we feel unsafe or untrusting. Self-trust and reclamation of our sovereignty are precursors for remembering to live in our bodies.

We'll also explore the final part of the KARE method: E—*engendering* ongoing remedies that support our healing, well-being, and reconciliation with our nuna, particularly through engagement with our full sentipensante and the hidden wisdom of the body.

In many ways, the process of coming back to ourselves and restoring balance can make people hypervigilant, as if they have to relinquish everything about their past in order to find harmony. However, weaving self-trust goes a lot deeper than adhering to external definitions of healing. Being in the body is a form of sentipensante. *Senti* relates to the experience of feeling the full spectrum of emotions and sensations that come from being in a body; *pensante* relates to the application of cognition to clarify our purpose and provide insight to catalyze inspired action. The *sentipensante* of being in our body with full awareness is a gift—and one that we can continue to cultivate throughout our lives. In fact, it is the most intimate and radical action we can take. It is a way of integrating our wholeness, or at least striving to, amid life's circumstances.

My hope is that you will experience your own intrinsic sense of sweetness. Regardless of how you may feel about yourself and your embodiment, you are alive on this Earth today because you are meant to be. As you water the seed that will sprout the meaning of your existence, as you continue your journey of healing and walk more decisively into joy, may your body be blessed.

WHERE DO YOU FEEL THE WOUND?

The body is where the jaguar resides. It may seem threatening or intimidating at first, but in truth, the jaguar is like a loving mother who is there to ferociously protect us, no matter how far we stray from ourselves. Fear and misunderstanding are common in our society and can contribute to becoming disconnected from our raw and primal nature, so it is easy to miss the mark when it comes to her intentions. Yes, the jaguar is confrontational, but this is in service of our growth. It challenges us to be emotionally honest with ourselves and to turn toward our fear rather than away. It guides us to fully inhabit our bodies and to pay attention to what needs tending to.

Of course, when we inhabit our bodies, it also becomes possible for us to cultivate greater understanding and sweetness, to be less reactive, and to address our distortions. From my work with clients, I have observed that a woman who steps into the profound initiation of "raising" and "breeding" herself becomes a strong thread in her community—with the capacity to braid robust, meaningful relationships that are in a state of constant growth. However, getting there means facing the jaguar.

I recall working with my client, Lila, who was a sailor in the Navy when I met her. She told me that she'd spent eight agonizing years going back and forth between deployments. Finally, she was called to duty in a city where she knew she could raise children. Her husband, Alex, was an attorney who could open his own practice while supporting his wife in her final act of duty with the Navy.

Lila came to me searching for ways to reduce her anxiety and depression, and to manage chronic pain. She explained, "I don't know if this is what being depressed looks like, but I'm definitely anxious, and sometimes I feel angry and sad at the same time."

She paused while fidgeting with her hands, which clued me in to how uncomfortable she felt. I felt my heart go out to her, as I knew it must be challenging for her to be so transparent.

She went on, "One of the things I think is making my life hard is that Alex and I have been trying to get pregnant for months, with no success. I don't know what's wrong with me."

I affirmed that I was happy Lila had come to me. As someone who'd struggled with my own chronic pain for many years, I could relate to her feelings—especially the sense of being both angry and sad. I also noted that in the chart she'd filled out before our session, she had written that she was tired of having chronic pain and that nothing she was doing helped.

"Lila, where do you feel the wound? Where are you hurting?" I asked.

She laughed sardonically. "Where don't I feel it? I don't remember the last time I wasn't in pain. Seriously, everything hurts."

I continued, "How old do you think this pain is? Is the pain yours?"

After a few breaths and a long pause, she sighed, "It feels very old. I think it's mine."

She went on to share her background. Lila had been the middle child and only girl in a conservative Christian family. She went to a private Christian school outside Washington, DC, where she played sports and had an active childhood. During her senior year of high school, Lila, who'd been a high-achieving and always-smiling girl, displayed signs of depression. The cause was heartbreak. Her then-boyfriend had decided to follow in his family's footsteps and join the Navy, just as his father and grandfather had. Lila grieved the absence of her boyfriend and cried every day, awaiting news from him. At the end of her final semester, she announced that she'd signed a four-year contract with the Navy in an attempt to be closer to her high-school sweetheart and make the pain go away, once and for all.

Lila was assigned to a ship that sailed the world. After a few years of being in a long-distance relationship with her boyfriend, where they'd meet up occasionally in overseas ports, he broke up with her. Lila felt her heart break all over again—not only because of the breakup, but because of the devastating sense of regret she had about following him and putting her own dreams on hold. The long hours of work and life on the ship, surrounded by hundreds of sailors, allowed her to build resilience and to forget about her heartbreak and the dreams that now felt lost to her forever.

As Lila and I continued to work together, that simple question—"Where do you feel the wound?"—unlocked old memories that she believed had been resolved, but that were actually hiding in plain sight inside the chronic pain, in the sadness and the anger, in the confusion and hurt she had no words for. I could see it in her body language, but it was more important for *her* to come to terms with it. So, that initial question became a basis for our exploration—and one that unlocked the possibility of healing. To ask it, to ourselves or another, is to say, "I want to know you—no filters. I want to pay attention to you, so that I can help you write the story of your healing."

Knowing about Lila's experience of suffering helped me to understand what was in her heart. Connecting with her on this level was natural to me because I have experienced my own share of pain and suffering. The same is true for many of my clients, especially Latina women who are learning to come back into a fuller and more emotionally honest relationship with themselves after decades of internalized abuse that caused them to put themselves last.

As Lila gradually came to learn, the body tells the story of our hurt, our disappointment, and the places where we might find it difficult to let life all the way in . . . where we might find it difficult to *feel*. At the same time, I want to be cautious about equating all kinds of pain with the kind that is manifested from our sentipensante into the layers of our body. There are many forms of pain that cannot be treated in the ways I'm suggesting and that would be better addressed by seeing a medical doctor. Please use your judgment in treating different forms of pain—exercise your autonomy and make the choice that's best for you!

There is an emotional pain that we carry that often manifests in our physical experience. This kind of pain, which often can't be related back to a cause by medical doctors, is hard to acknowledge. But as I learned, it is possible to love one's pain, as a teacher and a messenger that is always conveying important information. Of course, some of us, like Lila, have come to see pain as part of the backdrop of our lives, indistinguishable from everything else. Lila had developed a high tolerance for pain, but the inflection point—which came when she considered starting her own family—made the pain intolerable. Accordingly, all of us will experience a time when we cannot keep avoiding the pain and what it has to tell us.

Often, when I work with a client to identify and locate their pain and to determine where they stand in relation to it, we start to explore sacred boundaries, which we create when we take back our autonomy. Unsurprisingly, many of my clients who come to me share the experience of not just giving too much but of sacrificing themselves, body and spirit, in order to have connection with others. Also, many people end up carrying pain that isn't even theirs, because they have inherited the idea that caring for others means taking the burden of their suffering.

Honoring our pain means coming back into connection with ourselves, first and foremost. It means establishing clear boundaries that affirm our right to lead happy, healthy, balanced lives. This helps us recognize if we are in situations that exacerbate our pain or take us further away from ourselves. Essentially, learning to take back our autonomy is a process that requires unapologetic truth, radical intimacy, and the willingness to institute a mature and loving intervention with ourselves, especially if we've developed self-depleting habits.

Provided that you are not in debilitating pain that impacts your ability to function on a day-to-day basis, pain can sometimes help you establish intimacy with yourself. But first, you have to turn toward it. You have to gaze unflinchingly in the direction of the jaguar and recognize that she isn't there to eat you; she is there to bring you home.

THE BODY: A PORTAL TO NATURE

Engendering sustainable healing means recognizing the sacred importance of the body, which is our first and last home in this realm. This is why we must make it a safe place to come back to, so we can keep welcoming our nuna into its embrace. But how do we learn to build trust in ourselves when trust has been lost or compromised due to ongoing emotional and physical difficulties?

This entails a process of continually weaving ourselves back into the manta of belonging—in other words, engendering our own healing (the E in the KARE method). The pain, the aches, and the fears may still be there, but the way we choose to become proximate to them will transform—and thus, the way we experience them will change. Where we may have previously felt numbness and desolation, we will be grateful for a twinge in our limbs or a sharpness in our heart. Our apprehension will transform into a recognition of our primal nature, our aliveness, our tender vulnerability.

In other words, healing is not the same as transcending what is happening to us or moving beyond our feelings and emotions. Healing is not about pretending that pain is gone. It is about building a vocabulary that enables us to connect with the messages that are constantly being transmitted through our body. For example, if your shoulder hurts, you might have a sense that there is something else below the physical pain. When you face that pain with honor, you can ask what else is present. You might receive an answer like, "My physical body is getting older, and I know that pains and aches are part of aging, but the deeper pain here is telling me that I'll never be able to do the things I used to. I will be left out of my family's activities." This pain is precisely what Pacha can help you to reconcile. This is where you will enter the realm of the jaguar. You will develop the capacity to communicate with your feelings and emotions in ways that allow you to become more situated in the body, and to be in a state of loving dialogue with it.

Here, I want to distinguish between our feelings and our emotions. Emotions are like raw data, while feelings are our personal, internal reflections on that data. I view emotions as spirits that live under one roof. Every single one of them is in relationship with all the others, and it is our job to get proximate to all of them, even the ones that we wish to cast outside ourselves because we've been habituated to believe that they are "bad." If we are not emotionally equipped, which many of us are not, we might live with terror in the face of these sensations, which we cannot always define because we have not developed a sufficient relationship with them. If this continues to be the case, it isn't possible to come into a healthy relationship with the body or to make it a safe place for our nuna to come home. Ultimately, reconnecting with the body is about creating a home for all our emotions and corresponding feelings.

There are usually a handful of emotions that run our life. Sometimes we are moved by smooth emotions, but many times, we are moved by dense emotions. Dense emotions and smooth emotions are siblings under the same umbrella. According to the Pacha worldview, the totality of who we are is made up of a series of correlating opposites. For example, one of the dense emotions that has been a part of my reality for years is the experience of fear I often feel in the face of separation. This fear disconnects me from myself, from other people, and from Nature. I discovered through my spiritual work that human contact and connection is the best medicine. In fact, connection is the smooth emotion that lives on the other end of the spectrum from separation. Paradoxically, they are complementary and cannot exist without one another.

The dense emotion that tends to rule our life is usually the place where we most often need to experience healing. When I worked with Lila, she told me that although she felt she had done everything she could, she couldn't break out of a sense of constriction. She also felt an inexplicable sorrow that made her feel depleted and lifeless. I knew that this was the portal through which Lila's nuna was escaping and fragmenting.

I asked her, "What do you want, emotionally speaking?"

We spent several weeks on that question. Many people who carry painful emotions that tend to fragment them have seldom been asked what they want. Often, it may take them a while to answer. Together, Lila and I worked on cultivating more resources for her, including fortifying her relationship with Nature and the elements, as well as with her ancestors and the God of her understanding. Although the openness of my question felt intimidating to Lila, I gently reminded her that the answer to that question is usually very simple.

As we probed more deeply, Lila revealed that she felt overwhelmed. She had come to me with the idea that she wanted a family. In truth, she didn't know what she wanted. She had always prioritized other people's ideas about what she should want and who she should be.

"Why don't we start with what you actually *need* right now?" I asked. "Perhaps when you get what you need, you can start to reflect more on what you want."

We didn't get there right away, but it turned out that what she *needed* was spaciousness—to figure out whether becoming a mom was the next right step for her. In fact, spaciousness was the smooth emotion on the other side of constriction. In other cases, depending on the person and situation, they need to identify what they want in order to identify the need behind it. However, when someone says, as Lila did, that they don't know what they want, we can start with the need. And for Lila, by getting the need for spaciousness met, she could someday figure out what she wanted.

Our deepest, most primal want is often correlated to our needs, as I've discovered, which is why our needs can be a good place to start. However, I've also worked with clients who assure me that they know exactly what they want. Then, they'll say something like, "I want my partner to stop smoking." This is what I would call an unwholesome yearning, because it's focused on a specific outcome that is believed to be necessary in order to ensure happiness. It is connected to control rather than a life-affirming desire. In such cases, I try to help my client get to the deeper primal want—in this case, it might be the desire to see their partner flourishing and in good health, or the desire to grow old together, unencumbered by serious health conditions. When they get to this place, it becomes easier to see that there are many possible ways to fulfill that primal want.

As we worked to create more spaciousness in Lila's life, she identified that play and pleasure were actually her authentic desires. Lila had never known the deep-seated joy some part of her longed for, and this is true for many people. This is when it can be useful to work with metaphors, and with Nature itself. Language is often incomplete when it comes to telling our body's stories, but Nature tells us everything we need to know.

"I want to feel the kiss of the sunset," Lila wrote in her poetry. "When I see the butterfly dancing, I feel my own heart dance." Her ability to find solace in the everyday language of Nature helped her to reconnect with her primal state, which is where she reconnected with the sacredness of her body.

My hope is that one day we will all remember that our body is a portal to the sacred, through which our wisdom and the wisdom of our ancestors may flow. And when we learn to situate ourselves in the body, which is the home that holds all our memories and emotions and is also the cover of our nuna, our hearts will be safe and ready to heal. We will see that our bodies are the bridge between the seen and unseen realms. Like Lila, we will discover the indescribable sweetness of being, and the spaciousness that offers us permission to rest. We will remember that our body is just another part of Pacha, calling us home to all parts of our experience.

MIRROR THE JAGUAR

Making a Home for Your Emotions (KARE Method: Engender)

This exercise introduces the E of the KARE method: *engendering* ongoing remedies for our sense of connection to ourselves and our nuna.

- Pay attention to the experiences of emotional/physical pain that you tend toward, as well as where they live in your body. Identify your most common dense emotions, as well as the medicine, or the smooth emotion, that lives on the other side. This will be different for everyone. Perhaps your dense emotion is often feeling a searing loneliness. Knowing this will get you to the complementary smooth emotion. For example, on the other side of the spectrum from loneliness is a bubbly joy that is full of laughter and delight. You can engage with primal drawing, writing, or even dancing with respect to dense emotions. What are they conveying to you? Often, interacting with them opens the door to the smooth emotions on the other side.

- Make a home for your dense emotions. Imagine yourself creating a beautiful dwelling for them in the spirit realm, capturing the essence of what they want, so that they don't remain derelict or run roughshod over your life. If you wish, you can use drawing or crafts to make this house come to life. For example, using my imagination, I have built my dense emotions a house under the moon so that they can flourish here. I lovingly tell them, "Go and play under the stars and moonlight." In a primal drawing I made of this house, I made sure the door remained unlocked and open, to symbolize that my dense emotions can visit me from time to time, for I would not be human without them. I also try to bring my dense emotions gifts and offerings now and then, such as fruits and flowers. This helps me remember that I need to know the darkness in order to appreciate the light.

- Across cultures, "carnivals" are an opportunity to celebrate the pairs of opposites that make up our human experience—and in Pacha philosophy, everything is a celebration. Honor the full spectrum of your emotions, both dense and smooth, by taking time to celebrate—perhaps by dancing, wearing vibrant colors, or doing something to acknowledge the body as both a site of pain and pleasure. So, we aren't simply attempting to get back to homeostasis or a mere sense of safety in the body; we are remembering that we can also activate a sense of belonging in the process. Eduardo Galeano astutely observed, "The Church says: the body is a sin. Science says: the body is a machine. Advertising says: The body is a business. The Body says: I am a fiesta."[1]

TAKING YOUR AUTONOMY BACK

It's important to recognize that when we lose our bodily autonomy, that loss not only harms us, but also the entire community and ecosystem of which we are a part. In Quechua, the term *pishtaco* describes a phenomenon where someone's bodily autonomy is stolen, and is often portrayed as a kind of mythical "creature." This frightening force can steal our autonomy and nuna by stealing our human tissues and grease or fat.

During colonization, the people of Perú believed that the pishtaco used the fat or grease of human tissues to help Europeans make items that were beyond the ken of Indigenous peoples at the time. For example, they believed that the chains of the huge metal bells tolling in every church in every plaza must have been greased with a rare material like human fat. Even today, some believe that stolen human fat is needed to run new technology, from airplanes to laptop computers.

As I've studied the pishtaco stories over the years, I've come to believe there is both a metaphorical and literal dimension to it—an ambiguous, ever-mutable, and complex phenomenon that is much more than a superstitious folkloric vestige. In fact, it represents many aspects of power and violence that are familiar to the inhabitants of the Andean regions. In Perú, the stories passed down by generations tell the myth

---

1   Eduardo Galeano, *Las Palabras Andantes (Walking Words)* (Catálogos S.R.L., 1993), 109.

of the pishtaco, which was born when the foreign white men came to extract the fat of those who were living a reckless life or travelers who had lost their way.

The mythology around creatures like the pishtaco is still present among Indigenous communities today—where these creatures are manifestations of a justifiable anxiety that exploited communities may have about forces that intend to steal their autonomy. Such creatures are symbols of a deep-seated trauma that stretches across generations, holding genuine fears that were manufactured by brutal abuse for hundreds of years. These creatures are depicted as cannibalistic specters driven by an insatiable appetite that will stop at nothing to fulfill their ends—but through a more expansive perspective, we can see that they are misguided energies that are hungry and need to eat. They are constantly at war with the forces of Nature, so they represent a spiritual malaise that can easily take any of us under their spell—sometimes, by making us instruments of their wicked desires, forged in hunger, and causing us to justify our exploitation of other people and the natural world as a whole.

When I hear stories about the pishtaco, I recognize that so many of my ancestors felt powerless and subject to the whims and desires of those who had conquered them. They felt little to no autonomy over their bodies and destinies. The imprint of colonization, slavery, genocide, and brutal conquest has made itself known in the psyches of many people across the world, who were stripped of their sovereignty by forces that sought to dehumanize them.

Those who have experienced any kind of cruelty, mistreatment, and abuse understand that it can feel like it's been administered by a supernatural force. But the thing that connects conquistadors, converters, cold-blooded killers, and even well-meaning doctors is the very thing that makes the pishtaco legends most frightening of all: they are not supernatural, but human.

So, how do we reclaim our autonomy—not just from personal trauma, but from the societal and cultural forces that have historically served to quash our hopes and dreams, even now? Again, it is our responsibility to look for the medicine that will bring our autonomy back.

It can be very difficult to admit to our victimization when we've been harmed, but sometimes, recognizing where we have been victimized can help us to break out of it and reclaim our autonomy. Understanding all the intricate threads of our manta, which includes our personal history as well as the stories of our ancestors, is paramount. This is how we transform the mythic frightening creatures and the narratives that have kept us in a fog of fear and self-doubt.

Of course, all of this takes time, patience, and consistency. In those early years after reclaiming my body and my autonomy, my newfound empowerment was a double-edged sword. Everything became about *me*. I presented myself as an empowered woman who was a survivor, not a victim. I've seen many women go through this process, especially those who've encountered brutal violence. When they get a taste of their autonomy, it is understandable that they want to shout from the rooftops, declaring almost ragefully to the world, "No more of the past! It's my time to be me!"

It can feel intoxicating to take this stance, but if we are not careful, we might unknowingly become drunk on our own power. In fact, it is often true that the victim can turn into the perpetrator. Our righteous indignation can become a wrathful fire that incinerates anyone unlucky enough to get in the way.

While reclaiming sovereignty over our lives can be beautifully invigorating, we are not meant to merely thump our chests and declare ourselves survivors. Eventually, we must move past surviving and into flourishing. Flourishing is equivalent to recognizing our wholeness and grace without negating the bittersweetness of our journey and all we have been through. It requires coming into sacred balance with ourselves and the world, rather than using our past as an excuse to destroy whatever threatens us, which simply recapitulates old cycles of war and adversity.

The path of the jaguar is the path of the courageous. However, being an initiate on this path requires that we need to confront adversity when it is necessary, and we also need to know how and when to make peace and to coax new possibilities from the once-desolate soil of our hearts.

This also means giving ourselves permission to mourn, to be soft, to love, and to receive abundance with open arms.

REMEMBERING TO LISTEN, REMEMBERING TO TRUST

A few years ago, during a silent pilgrimage in the mountains, I engaged in a solo contemplation practice outdoors before dawn. Despite the fact that I knew there was no danger from large animals, I was overcome by a feeling of fear and imminent danger. As soon as I closed my eyes, my body shook. My heart raced, and I felt paralyzed. The fear was compounded by guilt and self-reproach, as if I had the power to control my feelings or external circumstances. My eyes fixed on a tree in front of me, and my fear intensified when I thought I saw the silhouette of a bear in the shadows. The mental and emotional battle to stay put despite the fear was exhausting, but I decided to embrace the fear with love and sweetness as I continued to focus on my breath and the sensations of the earth beneath me. As the sun rose, the silhouette of the bear I thought I saw dissolved into nothing.

Although the experience lasted less than twenty minutes, it felt like an eternity. I was initially shaken, but I felt proud that I was able to remain with what I felt. This experience allowed me to experience the roller-coaster ride of my nervous system. To this day, I'm grateful that Nature became my ally, weaving its steadfastness and wisdom through me, right in the midst of my experience.

I recognize that the capacity to be with oneself is connected to embracing the stillness and silence that lives inside, beyond the noise of our inner and outer world. However, maybe an indirect reason for the fear that arose within me is that silence was something I've historically had a difficult relationship with.

It took me time to recognize the effectiveness of intentional silence, of being quiet on purpose, so I could hear beyond the static of life and connect with the messages of my body that had remained a mystery for so long. But during my time on the mountain, I touched a potent moment of silence. Just as I had found freedom in the midst of my tears and sweat on that yoga mat so many years before, I was absolutely present, held by Nature. I knew that I could trust myself to *stay with me*.

This experience of learning to be with myself helped me to move from the darkest periods of debilitating melancholy, fear, and uncertainty. Many times, people ask me how I managed to do this, and the answer is elegant in its simplicity. I discovered that the beauty of peace and inner calmness are found in the most unadorned and unpretentious efforts, and in our capacity to appreciate the beauty of our world. It wasn't easy to rest into the wildness of the natural world, but as I sat there, intimate with my breath and my sentipensante, I stepped into the unapologetic truth—that I, too, was wild. I, too, was Nature resting in Nature. And opening up to this aspect made it so much easier to be with the part of myself that I'd once been scared of.

I love the experience of being woven back into Nature, because it helps me to step back into a sustainable root system of open receptivity. Sometimes, detaching from the external world can look like not watching the news, or consciously resisting superficial engagement with family members, friends, and colleagues. It can also look like sitting in Nature and watching the spiraling dance of the elements, or dancing in your pajamas to your favorite music. This process of making yourself a sanctuary, with open space for listening to and being with all dimensions of your sentipensante, is as unique as you are.

I cannot emphasize enough that consciously deciding to care for your well-being and to understand your emotional landscape is not the same as being oblivious or willfully ignorant about what is happening in the world. It doesn't mean that you're not a caring human who doesn't consider the pain and suffering of others. On the contrary, nourishing yourself and deepening into your inner silence, which you will find at the center of all the internal messages and the tangled web of emotions, is one of the most courageous, radical, and raw sacred contracts you can make to bring yourself back into wholeness. When you take this approach, your heart and mind are at peace; they become the sanctuary to which your nuna might return. You agree to care for your needs, and you do your part in promoting peace and harmony, knowing that many wars can be stopped when the inner self is attended to and validated.

As we close this chapter, beloved friend, I want you to know that it's okay to take a pause and to rest in your favorite manta. It's okay to take a break from the news. It's okay to be off the grid. It's okay to comfort the parts of you that still feel wired or jumpy. Taking the time to emotionally and mentally replenish yourself will weave you back into a sacred calmness that the world desperately needs. Over time, and with intention, practice, and perseverance, you will be a living embodiment of the stillness and silence that exist in the center of the maelstrom. This is what it means to practice sweet, unapologetic truth and radical intimacy. This is what it means to make a mature intervention that helps you respond to emotional exhaustion or residual fears that live in the body.

Don't worry if this process feels confusing or disorganized. Many of us are accustomed to living inside the noise of our and the world's fear, and feeling overwhelmed and disembodied from our experience. It takes practice to continue to come back to ourselves, to listen to the many messages that want to be heard, and to connect with the mystical quietude that is waiting for us . . . that is here to tell us that we can be a safe space for all of who we are. When we do this, we turn our body into a sanctuary.

We will know true sovereignty when we can feel safe with ourselves. To discern whether we're there yet, we can ask ourselves, "Would I send my children, elders, or sick relatives to myself with confidence that I'd accompany and care for them?"

Tell me, beloved friend, are you a safe space and a sanctuary?

EMBODY THE JAGUAR

Listening to Your Pain (KARE Method: Engender)
This exercise engages with the E of the KARE method: *engendering* ongoing remedies for our sense of connection to ourselves and our nuna.

- Take a deep breath. Recognize where you are. Feel all the places of innermost discomfort in your body. Say hello to them, being extra gentle, sweet, and attentive toward them, as they may not always make themselves known.

- Take your time asking each sensation whether it is yours or not, how old it is, and what it has to share with you. Thank them for however much they wish to share. You may wish to record the answers through freewriting or drawing. Allow the sensations to come from the most primal parts of you. Don't worry if they don't make any sense or if what you receive is filled with metaphors you may not understand. Our pain carries deep wisdom that we can receive if we open up to listening and letting it come through.

- Acknowledge your dense emotions. And if it feels right, ask them what they want and need. Maybe they request a nap, or for you to wear a favorite outfit. If it doesn't feel like the right moment to gather this information, let them know that you will revisit them in due time.

When you accompany your pain and discomfort, you will feel the loving embrace of the jaguar, reminding you that you can be a haven for your own healing. And this is how you will become proximate to your own nuna—by coming back to the sacred home of your body.

6
MOVING BEYOND INTERNALIZED DOMINATION

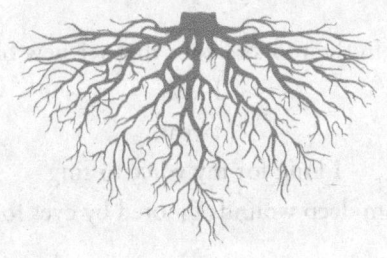

Let's Free Us Now

Two centuries later, I give thanks for the freedom
where the yoke no longer subdues.

For freedom, we cried.
For freedom, we gave our sweat.
For freedom, the people sang.

Time heals the backs of my ancestors.
With gratitude for their tenacity, I stand.

Today, braided in the roots of oaks that see new blood displaced,
I cry.
I sweat.
I long for my voice to sing
freedom songs from deep wounds ignored by eyes foreign to our pain.

I agree with the sovereignty of territories,
with the sense of independence classrooms preach.
Yes, I agree
but is that true freedom?

It's the release of tears from mothers who didn't birth me,
the anger reshaped into rebellion from fathers who didn't engender me,
this is the freedom I seek.

Delving into the legends of history
is a task from my sacred emotional memory,
which calls me to explore with shovel and pickaxe in hand.

From three hundred years of physical chains, they freed me.
From five hundred years of invisible wounds, it is time to free myself.

How long will it take you
to find the balm to heal
what makes you cry without knowing why?

Time waits for no one.

Please cry.
Please sweat.
Free yourself.

Sing songs of anger born from your womb,
reshaped into rebellion
and reconciled into peace.

Learning to trust ourselves and develop a strong relationship with the body as well as the environment in which we live, either where our seed was planted or where it was re-planted, is crucial. But even when we are successful at this, we may still feel ill at ease, due to the internalization of many forms of abuse and misguided energies that become poisonous to our sentipensante, so that our sense of autonomy is reduced or taken away.

This is where, despite the work we've done, we can get caught in the clutches of internalized domination. I define *internalized domination* as a process that's ongoing, both within us and in the societies and cultures we inhabit. Domination has occurred at different points throughout our human history in the external world—in scenarios like colonialism, civilizing missions, conquest of land, slavery, and the raping of the Earth. And it is still occurring, although the context may change according to time and place. But domination also happens inside us, when we are in the web of comparison, control, and hierarchy.

When we internalize domination, we see ourselves as inhabiting a place on a pyramid, where we're either on top of or below someone or something else, including Nature. For many of us, as well as our ancestors, this diminishes our integrity, our sense of safety, our autonomy, and our sentipensante. We become loose threads in the collective manta, disconnected from Nature. This influences how we treat ourselves, others, and Nature. It is also what imposes rules and standards that compromise our interconnectedness and lead to structural unfairness and biases.

On some level, there's a part of us that knows autonomy isn't about domination. It isn't about reaching for our power at someone else's expense. However, many of us have internalized the abuse that permeates the world of consensus reality, which includes ideas about who is worthy and deserving versus who isn't, so that it becomes hard for us to fully be with and in ourselves. It becomes hard for us to claim our overall sovereignty—especially because spiritual and emotional sovereignty is so different from the sovereignty of "me and only me" disconnection that seems to dominate our societies.

One way out of internalized domination is the creation of bridges between ourselves and Nature. When I was researching for and writing this book, and in my daily prayers and intentions, my pledge was and is: "May I be a safe bridge for those I encounter, guiding them toward whatever they need most in their life pilgrimage. May I be a safe bridge between mind and heart, body and spirit, knowledge and mystery. May I be a safe bridge that connects others to themselves and their sentipensante—a bridge that unites rather than divides."

The bridge is an important symbol because it depicts our interconnectedness. It helps us, as well, to reconnect with forgotten realities that have become less conspicuous to us—especially as our social and cultural norms, and our ways of addressing the grace, wholeness, and holiness of life, have mutated into mental fixations of scarcity, survival, and one-upmanship.

Internalized domination generally has four tones: The first is superiority, which usually comes when we feel that others are low on the "pecking order." The second is inferiority, whereby we might negate some aspect of ourselves because we believe we're "less than." But when someone stands in and honors their unapologetic truth and worth, there is no need to feel superior or inferior to anyone else. The third is saviorism, where we might seek to help others whom we secretly see as "less than." Often, our intentions are good, but we are still stuck in the hierarchy and aren't seeing clearly. Finally, there is the desire for liberation, which comes from the awareness of domination. Here, we might recognize that the hierarchy of "up" and "down" has dictated our entire life, and we want out of it. Many times, when we are here, we're tired of the struggle. We want to reclaim our gifts and shrug off the shackles.

I know that for myself, imposter syndrome has been an especially important lesson reminding me of where I've been uprooted from my sovereignty. In my early stages of being an entrepreneur, I often felt like a fraud, afraid that others would eventually discover my perceived inadequacies. I did everything I could to be seen as successful in the eyes of other people. Years later, I internalized a new story—one in which I was a trailblazer who could validate and accept my unique strengths and accomplishments, no matter what anyone else might have expressed to me. After so many years of salt being placed in my wounds, I recovered my sense of autonomy. I also realized that our narratives of internalized domination place a veil between us and our intrinsic nature, so that we can't experience our full capacity—even when we do great things in the world.

It wasn't until I went through the entire KARE method that I was able to embrace my true worth—not just because I had overcome seemingly insurmountable odds, but because the process allowed me to remember gifts that had been buried within me. And now, they were coming into fruition. I hope that you will discover, through your own healing efforts and work with the KARE method, that you are ready to shrug off the shackles of internalized domination for good, and to actualize your gifts—which will be the central focus of the next few chapters.

Although this is not an easy or pleasant topic, my intention is to awaken you to the brutal impacts of internalized domination, so that you can reclaim the seeds that have been buried within you. We're in a ripe time to claim our sovereignty. These days, so many of the systems of power that exist all around us are shaking and breaking. There are so many people taking a stand for widespread, fair, unbiased structures that prevent disparities, so that all of us can reconnect with our true worth—and so all of us can be held in a collective that enables our social structures to arrive into balance and interconnectedness.

In truth, although we are experiencing a reckoning on a collective level, all of it begins with *us*. We are downloads of animating force and wisdom that come directly from our ancestors. We literally came into being because of their efforts and dreams, which ushered us into this plane of existence. So, I want you to be assured that even if it feels like you are fighting an uphill battle to fully self-realize in a world that may not seem to have a place for you, you have more support than you can possibly know.

Simply trust that you are exactly where you need to be. And the time is coming for a large-scale metamorphosis that will catalyze you and all beings on this Earth to fully claim the intrinsic, graceful nature of who we are.

PLAYING FIFTY YEARS OF CATCH-UP

In many discussions about unbiased societal and structural fairness, we often hear the word *privilege*. When we refer to privilege, we're addressing an advantage that benefits those who belong to particular groups. Sadly, this word has created a boiling point for division. While it is a useful concept for many, it triggers others, which can make it difficult to have important, unbiased conversations about overall sovereignty and balance that all of us should be having.

While it's imperative to find an empathetic way into these difficult conversations, the *yoke of privilege* is very real. It can be defined as the burden that is carried by the inheritance of abuse, whether we come from people who were perpetrators or those who were victims. In fact, both are braided into our lineages. The yoke can feel like a burden, though, which makes it difficult to bear its weight. At the same time, it shouldn't result in pointing fingers. Rather, we can come to see with clarity and discernment all the ways we may be living inside a cycle of abuse, as well as all the ways we have hurt and been hurt by others.

Many people with Indigenous backgrounds around the world, including those of *la tierra viva* or "the land in full bloom" (a translation of Abya Yala, an Indigenous neologism for the Americas), experienced hundreds of years of domination and decimation of our cultures. This was accompanied by brutalities such as exploitation and subjugation, a nearly complete stripping-away of our Indigenous cultures, extraction from our lands, the enslavement of African people, and many other wounds. At the same time, both the blood of the colonizer and the colonized run through the veins of so many of us.

Seeing the factual reality of our social structure with clarity requires us to hold this complexity. As we look at the ways we internalize domination, it's important to recognize how it can harm our sentipensante—whether we're in the "privileged" position or not.

One of the consequences of living under the lingering effects of colonization and internalized domination is that so many people across the world, not just Abya Yala, are playing a game of "catch-up." Indigenous time is very different from the dominant Western model of time and progress. This means that many of us who hail from Indigenous traditions have become separated from them in the furious race to the "top." This is the race to mold ourselves into the dominant culture, because we've been systematically inculcated with the belief that we are substandard if we don't.

Ironically, although this vision of success may push some people to catch up with industrialized cultures, mainstream spirituality is moving in a completely different direction. Today, there are people in the industrialized Western world drifting in the direction of pre-industrial knowledge and "timeless" Indigenous values—not just in their spiritual practices, but even in efforts toward environmental conservation. Certainly, if you're a person with Indigenous roots or someone who comes from colonized lands, all of this can be disorienting. Throughout history, our ways of thinking and being, our very sentipensante, were nearly eradicated, and in many cases, we have been considered uncivilized savages rather than human beings. However, we were resilient enough to protect, collect, and keep some of our knowledge. And although our knowledge is now perceived as valuable, we still receive mixed messages about our worth. So, even if we're now being informed that our traditions and knowledge are important, it doesn't take away from the fact that Indigenous lands have been ravaged by traumatic events that left their imprint.

Ultimately, systems like colonization and civilizing missions, which were built on domination, have long-lasting harmful effects that perpetuate global harm and division, from which we all suffer. Our current programming is centered around the ideals of the dominant culture—around "power" in the form of money, comfort, and influence.

Those inducted into industrialized culture are harvesting the consequences of factors like climate change and shifts in social and political policies. Due to this, many people are mobilizing and, in some ways, escaping. This phenomenon occurs across all social strata. There is a growing population of expatriates who have the financial resources to relocate to lands where they can rebuild their lives. In such places, they may be able to create their own exclusive communities where they are able to enforce their own rules. This is detrimental to locals who might face a rise in the cost of living, as their birthlands are reshaped to accommodate newcomers' needs, among other consequences. However, they must also go through their own reconciliation process to admit that something within the larger systems from which they're relocating is breaking.

While those expatriates with financial resources—most of them from Western countries—are moving toward "luxurious comfort," many others from non-Western cultures are leaving everything behind to find "success." This perpetuates a toxic cycle in which those who have less remain behind.

There is a remedy for this game of catching up. People who hail from industrialized nations, which tend to be the shapers and controllers of culture, are invited to pause and walk backwards, following the nonlinear progression of Indigenous time toward their own roots. And those who have been attempting to keep pace with the speed of industrialization can similarly strive to integrate industrial innovations that can change our societies for the better.

If we strive for harmony and unbiased structures that prevent disparities, we must form a genuine relationship with the natural world and one another in order to overcome the domination that has impacted all of us on some level. Together, we might learn to see how all of us have experienced a devastation of our original cultures around the world, which saw the Earth as sacred, rather than as a commodity to be used and abused.

As we do the work to reconnect with Nature, we can come to a deeper understanding of what it might mean to be with one another—not attempting to have power over anyone or anything but cultivating the ability to move in harmony toward our mutual healing.

MOVING BEYOND VICTIM AND PERPETRATOR

Ultimately, it's not enough to simply understand where we've been. We also have to consider where we are going. If we want to heal, that means we must learn to move beyond the roles of victim and perpetrator. After all, internalized domination includes both the mentality of the dominator, as well as that of the dominated. There are places within us where we cower from cruelty, as well as places within us where we are the ones wielding the whip.

As we consider what it means to disentangle from the domination that lives within us and is reflected collectively, it's useful to come back to the image of the jaguar. Once we are on the journey to reclaiming our autonomy, it's almost as if we're walking on the legs of the jaguar. In a way, this places us in a privileged position, because we are a predator at the top of the food chain, relatively speaking. However disturbing this image might be, autonomy always brings with it a sense of responsibility as we consider that many people never achieve it.

If you are reading this book, it is likely you have *some* degree of privilege and autonomy. You probably have the means and resources to seek healing, and you also most likely have some influence over the circumstances of your life. The point of recognizing your privileged position isn't to guard it or justify why you have it. At the same time, an aspect of undoing the tangles of internalized domination is that we can use our autonomy to ensure that we flourish collectively.

Using our advantageous status to guide others can sometimes mean that we inadvertently exercise a savior mentality. A person who stands in the position of savior may fall into the trap of believing that only *they* have the knowledge and awareness to take others where they need to go. The problem with this approach is that it tends to maintain a hierarchy of status. This attitude can also generate greed and corruption. It perpetuates inferiority and superiority complexes, as well as chronic self-doubt. It causes us to forget that our true wealth transcends material comfort and technological progress.

If you've ever experienced guilt or shame about your privileged position and the advantages in your life, it's a good idea to face these emotions and feelings with understanding and truthfulness. Just as we explored our dense emotions in chapter 5, you can ask them, "What do you need? What do you want?" Hearing them out and giving them a safe space in which to "play" is a part of learning to be with all parts of yourself, especially the ones that exist in a state of inner conflict. It is very important to face the conflict within us head-on if we wish to co-create a more harmonious world.

In using our position in life to even out the disparities we see around us, we will inevitably come to the spiritual understanding that there are two sides to every coin. Each of these sides may even be part of a cycle that is necessary to our self-actualization. After all, according to Pacha philosophy, power cannot exist without its complementary opposite: defeat. Just like Nature, power is part of an ever-changing cycle—one day you will have it, and other days you will not. Power is a system in constant rotation, and no matter what our efforts are, there will always be someone or something ahead of us. There is no true "up" or "down," because our positions are in a state of constant flux.

As soon as we see that all of us are moving along the wheel, we can re-embrace our multifaceted self. We can cultivate humility, whether we stand in a privileged position or not. This can extend beyond the ways we treat one another and to the natural world itself, which most humans have exploited and taken for granted.

MIRROR THE JAGUAR
Reconciling with Structural Biases

- Where are your original ancestors from? If you belong to more than one racial/ethnic/geographic group, go with the one you feel closest to.

- What are the messages you have received about your ancestry? As a result, how do you feel about it? Do you carry pride, shame, or mixed emotions?

- If you belong to an underrepresented group, have you chosen to hide parts of your identity in order to fit into a dominant group? Based on some of the ideas you've internalized, do you suppress your differences or embrace them? How can you exercise awareness around the places where you may be hiding in order to thrive?

- Are there any stereotypes you've internalized due to familial and societal expectations? Many stereotypes tend to be contradictory, especially depending on where they get applied. For example, I've been bombarded by stereotypes about Latinas being submissive underachievers and caretakers—but also hypersexual, hot-tempered, loud, and obnoxious. In what ways have you succumbed to or resisted such stereotypes?

- Many of us carry aspects of both exploited and exploiter within us, in ways both tangible (e.g., having Mestizo ancestry that carries both Indigenous and European blood) and less tangible (e.g., being part of an underrepresented group while holding status, perhaps in the form of monetary wealth). Can you identify the ways in which you may carry both?

- If you belong to the dominant culture of your society in several respects, how do you look at those who don't? Do you see them as "less than"? Are you curious about their cultures and their ways of being in the world? Do you feel guilty about your own privileged position and the advantages in your life? In what ways can you seek to be an advocate rather than a savior? Remember that such attitudes can lurk just below the surface of good intentions.

- In what ways are you in a privileged position? Again, please remember that if you're reading this book, you likely are (to some degree) in a privileged position. How would you like to use your position to serve others?

THE PRINCIPLES OF SUMAQ KAWSAY

Many Indigenous cultures have sustained themselves for generations through powerful traditions and social practices that actually made them very advanced—not the primitive, backward civilizations that invading forces made them out to be, which, in many cases, they used to justify the act of conquest.

In numerous Indigenous cultures across the planet, the thread of sustenance was broken through violent conquest. It seems to be true that if you want to break a people, you use violence against them until it becomes internalized; until it becomes the unconscious language that spreads its poison through their veins.

There is a fascinating Quechua concept known as *Sumaq Kawsay*, which translates to "well living." It is premised on the understanding that all cycles eventually recede, and in order to have true wellness, we must institute methods that promote harmony with self, others, and Nature as a whole. Sumaq Kawsay is a set of guidelines for living in sacred reciprocity with the planet, encompassing all the animals, plants, elements, and even our *sentipensante*. It helps us to flourish in such a way so that we are not simply reacting to domination, whether it is internal or external. Sumaq Kawsay is practiced throughout the Andean region, especially in recognizing the personhood of Nature, which is the animating force of our earthly reality.

Rich in remarkable synergistic codes that aim for a sustainable lifestyle, Sumaq Kawsay points out five profound principles that support our pilgrimage to move beyond internalized domination and bring ourselves in sync with Nature.

The first principle is *relationality*. According to this principle, everything in existence has its own nuna. And even problems and difficult emotions are our relatives. How are we relating to everything in existence? How proximate are we to all that surrounds us, internally and externally? This idea of relationality removes us from the hierarchical structures that tend to be an aspect of our daily reality. Rather than a "you're up and I'm down" mentality, relationality encourages us to coexist on a continuum in which we are all embraced by Nature. After all, we are interwoven in the fabric of existence, whether we wish to be or not.

The second principle is *complementarity*, the idea that every aspect of our reality can be understood and explored through its interplaying opposite, so that both sides work together to create a balanced, complete whole. We live in a world of dualities, made of pairs of opposites that are equal and inseparable. For example, each of us carries both feminine and masculine qualities, essential to our human experience. These opposite fields of energy connect with one another and cannot be disconnected, as they are part of the same reality supporting balance and union. Complementarity is the recognition that we do not live in isolation. Accordingly, each of our dense and smooth emotions has a complementary emotion on the other end of the spectrum, which helps us to experience the full complexity of our human experience.

The next principle is *correspondence*. Correspondence is a way to read or navigate the interconnected world shaped by complementarity. We exist in a field of opposites that mirror or reflect each other within a broader system. We carry both micro and macro realities, just as we carry both light and dark, victim and perpetrator—two sides that are always different but mutually dependent.

This dynamic relationship shows how opposing elements can correspond and relate across layers, mirroring, and patterns, maintaining balance and continuity.

Next, we have the principle of *reciprocity*, which is about sacred balance. We give and we receive, and in so doing, we recognize that harmonic balance is a prerequisite to living well. By no means do we take more than we need, and we give what is in our capacity to give. We understand that the greatest gift of all is life, and our pilgrimage upon this Earth is an attempt to honor this gift as best as we can, with the same grace that the Creator afforded us.

Finally, we have the principle of *cyclicality*. This gives us the ability to situate ourselves in current time, and to project ourselves into the future based on what has already occurred. Cyclicality could be represented as a spiral, where everything is in motion. Being part of this spiral also means understanding that everyone and everything within it can recognize what comes next and what is being left behind. Cyclicality in all forms of Pacha is a phenomenon of rhythmic perfection and reorientation. From this notion arises the idea that we must look to the past to know where we are going. This challenges the limited idea of the straight line of constant progress. Instead, progress has a natural rhythm of renewal, decay, and regeneration, as opposed to constant, uninterrupted advancement. This approach suggests that change and evolution are more complex, requiring adjustments, pauses, or even setbacks. In Andean thought, humans have the capacity to course-correct imbalances through the celebration of sacred contracts and by reorienting themselves in the cycle they are in.

Essentially, Sumaq Kawsay is a set of guidelines and an ancient knowledge that transcends the Inca people. It doesn't belong to Perú alone, but to the entire Andean community and the region as a whole. It is so expansive and ancient that these pages cannot possibly do justice to this fascinating philosophy! All of the precepts of Sumaq Kawsay are extremely important when we look at what it means to live in our world today, where so many people feel bereft of connection. This is true whether we are a person who does not have a deep sense of relationship to our ancestry or we're carriers of Indigenous heritage who have witnessed our cultural practices being treated as commodities.

All of us are invited into the responsibility of moving toward cultural reconciliation and shrugging off the shackles of internalized domination. Sumaq Kawsay gives us a way to heal the wounds that divide us—internally and externally, with one another and collectively. With the principles of relationality, complementarity, correspondence, reciprocity, and cyclicality, we become more proximate to Nature. We can see it and ourselves as we truly are: an exquisite manta into which all the complex elements of life are woven. We recognize that when our sister the whale loses her children due to the crime of overharvesting the ocean, all of us lose something essential. By acknowledging that the trees are our cousins, we become more thoughtful about how we are treating them and what we are taking from them.

Sumaq Kawsay allows us to unmask the lies that oppressive systems have handed down to us, including the idea that humans are the masters of the planet. Of course, there is sorrow involved in such clarity, but it is a small price to pay, considering the suffering that we have inflicted upon ourselves and the natural world by severing our sentipensante from the multidimensional principles of well living. Beloved friend, all the practices in this book are meant to give you tools for well living, in your own life and in your communities.

THE ROLE OF SACRED ANGER AND FORGIVENESS

As a society, we are in the midst of awakening from the nightmare of trauma, and because of this, there is a great deal of anger that we are collectively feeling. Many of us are only now beginning to grasp the collective wrongdoings that have brought us to what seems to be a boiling point in our current human era. But how long will it be this way? How long will we maintain a state of explosive anger?

As a manta keeper and receiver, I believe it's my sacred duty to provide essential resources and guidance to those who are entering the emotional and spiritual battlefield in which they can call back their nuna, face and embody the jaguar, and come back to life. With my KARE method, my hope is that I can aid people in reconciling with themselves and awakening the wisdom that is not merely predicated on our collective wounding. I believe it's extremely important to acknowledge everything that happened in the past continues to impact us in the present. But we cannot change the past. I can't change the fact that colonizers came, raped the grandmothers of my grandmothers, killed millions in their quest for wealth, destroyed cultures, and imposed fear-based structures that came to dominate entire regions.

Many of us have never properly wept for our ancestors and for the destruction of our cultures through domination and force. Whether our ancestors were the dominators or the dominated doesn't change the outcome; they all paid a price that led to greater disconnection from the manta of creation.

But now, the jaguar is calling for us. It is time for us to grieve and to heal. So much anger has been accumulated in our spiritual and emotional stream, but it is time to seek reconciliation and healing from all the multidimensional realms. Otherwise, we run the risk of doing to others exactly what has been done to us.

The process of healing is about reclaiming our spiritual and emotional sovereignty, but we can only do this from a harmonious place, not a wounded place in which we continue to writhe in the aftermath of suffering. We are all being called to embody the jaguar and to recognize that our ancestors are not dead and gone—they continue to live through us.

We've known war and battle since the beginning of civilization; many will argue that conflicts have shaped the course of the human species. The fact is, there is a great deal of accumulated hurt, but getting to peace isn't about spiritually bypassing our way into good feelings. Rather, we must face our anger. We must allow it to motivate us, while remembering that anger can sometimes be a dense emotion. If we entertain it for too long, it can lead to fragmentation. At the same time, anger is a valuable ancestor, a spirit who needs to eat—so we must feed it nourishing food, which will allow it to guide us to do what we are here to do.

Anger is a primal emotion that is sometimes very challenging to feel and visit, but underneath it, we can find a great deal of information that will guide us to move forward in inspiring and impactful ways. For me, and many of the women I work with, anger has been an incredible motivator. It was a guardian and part of my survival spirit for a long time.

At the same time, I have fought for too long, and I don't want to fight anymore. I choose to make a mature intervention with my privileged position by understanding my responsibility. In honoring anger and those who are carrying it for the collective, it's vital to recognize its spirit. We can do this in sacred contracts that tend to our dear relative, anger—especially anger that has gone neglected and has run amok in the same way a child who has not been given love and attention might wreak havoc on the world around them.

Going back to some of the questions we explored in chapter 5, it is possible to make contact with your anger so that you're in a healthy and wholesome relationship with it. You can ask your anger the questions: "What do you need? What do you want?"

When you ask these questions with radical intimacy and unapologetic truth, you might be surprised to hear anger respond with, "I need a hug." This is the aspect of anger whose needs have been unattended, perhaps because you either restrained it or let it explode in ways that were not skillful or honest. However, when you are able to fulfill the needs of anger—which is often a signal that your boundaries have been violated—you can ask what it actually wants. Anger can give you much information about its yearning when its needs are met. Perhaps it will tell you that it wants justice and peace; that it wants a world in which people get to live freely and safely.

When you ask these questions, you will also learn what your anger is fighting for, and this will give you autonomy to respond with a mature intervention. This way, you aren't simply allowing your anger to spread like a wildfire that leaves everything in its wake destroyed. In truth, the energy of anger is extremely mobile and powerful, like an untamed fire, and we are meant to work with it, not to eradicate it.

Our quest is also to recognize that anger lives by the principle of complementarity. According to Sumaq Kawsay, in order to work well with anger, we must increase the other side of it, which is peace. It is possible to cherish conflict and peace, side by side. In addition, being brave in this time requires that we embody our own unique guardian spirit. For example, you don't have to force yourself to follow others who might be nourishing their anger in specific ways. Perhaps people in your life suggest you take a stand in a particular manner, but your sentipensante tells you this isn't right for you at the moment.

Overall, as we work with the principle of complementarity, we will learn to accept that anger, when it is expressed through violence and division, is not the way forward. The medicine that we need can only be found through the heart and from cooperation with all of life. The danger of living in a world that has so much unhinged anger is that we are usually taught to wield it with skill, instead of visiting it with sweetness and grace to understand where this anger is coming from. This is why we must turn to the wisdom traditions of our ancestors, which may include working with the elements in order to be with difficult states in our sentipensante.

Because I intend for this book to be a gift to the women who will eventually become the matriarchs of their societies and communities, I wish for you, beloved friend, to practice moving through anger in ways that support all of us to create the world we want for our grandchildren. It strikes me that most movements that center on social fairness and balance are well-intentioned, but often end up taking us further from the very thing we say we want most. Anger can initiate us into action, but it carries a volatile essence that may stop short of transformation.

Of course, one of the most critical aspects of learning to work with anger is remembering to welcome forgiveness. Without forgiveness, the pilgrimage to anger would be incomplete. In order to know forgiveness, we must be familiar with hurt and suffering. As we make the journey that our anger has bred from the flames that line the side of the road, we must recognize that the purpose of the road is forgiveness.

Forgiveness does not condone or justify the wrongdoing toward us; instead, it guides us to understand that we are all children of the same Earth, sharing an experience that each of us takes part in weaving. I believe that the ultimate destination of our collective journey, especially if we are choosing to move beyond resentment and systems of domination, is to experience and embody forgiveness. Forgiveness is the spirit that enables the dance of unity on this planet. It allows the Earth to continue giving us crops despite overly extractive agricultural practices, and it moves us around the sun.

For me, the season of autumn offers an extremely clear vision of forgiveness. When I attempt to internalize forgiveness, I think of the tree losing its leaves in preparation for a long winter. Bittersweetness fills my heart. It reminds me that the trees willingly become naked. They understand that there is a cycle they must go through in order to get to the other side. In a way, forgiveness is a recognition of the cycle that brings us full circle back to love, and the sweetness of new life.

Of course, I have numerous clients who have existed in their autumn season for years rather than months. They tell me, "There's no way I can forgive. I'm so angry. I feel low and lost. I don't think I'll ever recover from this."

But the truth is, as Pacha philosophy tells us, all cycles come to an end. All of us will eventually get to forgiveness—perhaps not now, but someday, sometime. I believe this is also what our ancestors are waiting for. They want forgiveness for their wrongdoings against our human and nonhuman relatives. They also want us to accept our responsibilities as custodians of our lineage and the Earth. This is why we must learn how to embody forgiveness. However, the pilgrimage forward for each of us will be unique.

Forgiveness is not something that we necessarily do out of volition. It is the completion of the cycle. It is the reward of the spring that comes when we allow the blossoming to occur in its own time. But we must allow the other spirits, such as anger, fear, and sadness, to come out; we must visit and play with them in order to reach forgiveness.

You'll know when you're able to truly forgive someone or something when you can sit with it and it no longer hurts you. My hope is that we can all learn to forgive one another and find ourselves resting beneath the same tree. But of course, forgiveness is ongoing. We can do it by starting with the smaller aspects of our lives. We may not be ready yet to forgive the abuser who has harmed us the worst. Until we get there, we can begin forgiving in other ways. For example, perhaps we can seek the forgiveness of the plant we didn't water for nearly two weeks. We can look at the subtle acts of hostility and domination that we carelessly inflict, recalling that we hold both victim and perpetrator within us.

It can also be useful to look at perpetrators as energy that exists beyond their human suit, not just as individuals who were acting from knowledge or true volition. What is the misguided energy they represent in the collective? How can we call back our nuna so that we feel more fortified to forgive them? In what ways can the driving force of domination come to rest so that it is folded back into the dance of existence; so that all of us can reconcile with the wounds that have served to fragment us from ourselves and one another? And with our forgiveness, how can we make the world whole so that we are courageous enough to write a new story and weave a new manta?

EMBODY THE JAGUAR
A Dialogue Between Anger and Forgiveness

- How do anger and forgiveness feel in your body? Where in your body is each emotion located? If it feels difficult for you to experience anger, consider a time when you felt rage in the face of a boundary violation. If it feels difficult for you to experience forgiveness, consider a time when you experienced the greatest holiness you have ever known. Overall, if the idea that you can be home to both anger and forgiveness seems far-fetched, consider how Nature continues to supply all of life with abundance, even in the face of poor treatment—and also, how it can focus its rage in primal expression. Refer to the graphic from chapter 3 to write down where the feeling lives in your body.

- Allow yourself to enter an intimate, self-reflecting space in which anger and forgiveness can literally speak to each other. First, you must allow yourself to feel each of them in your body; perhaps, for you, forgiveness lives in your heart and anger lives in your gut. You can also do some primal freewriting, using your non-dominant hand to write out these emotions' responses to one another. How does anger feel toward forgiveness, and vice-versa? How do they wish to coexist?

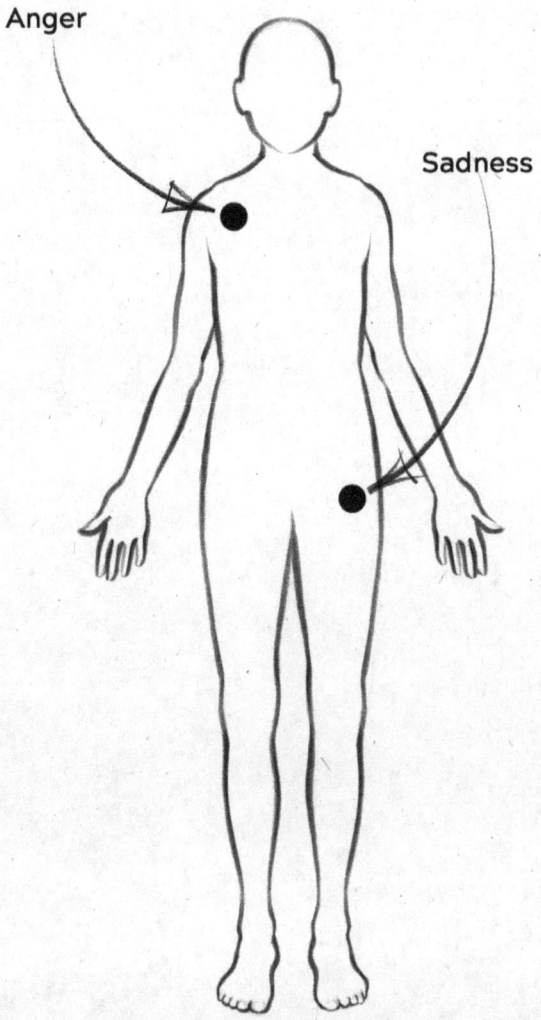

Our physical body holds the imprints of significant life experiences, storing emotions like sadness, anger, hope, etc. in specific areas. By mapping where these feelings reside in the body, we begin the journey of reconnecting with ourselves and others, opening a pathway to healing and integration.

7

HEALING THROUGH LINEAGE

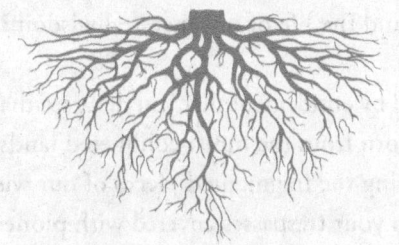

Abuelita's Scolding

I am tired of overarching my life
constantly making my truth easy for your limited narrative to consume.

My grandmothers' message is
not another fancy picture you can take to decorate your wall,
is not a creed for you to reduce as a slogan
and live by while expanding your green domains.

How dare you tell me how to live the truth of my life
and the life of my ancestral wisdom?

Are you so blinded by entitlement that you don't see that my sisters and I,
born from the moist conquered lands,
are using the fragmented pieces of our wisdom
in response to your trespasses covered with pioneers' glamour?

Since your blindness for power is as big as the rivers
made of the blood of those before me,
I am telling you today that in my exhaustion
from trying to keep up with you,
the claws and voice of my jaguar are waking up to roar.

***

Suddenly, the Abuelita woke and spoke:
"Oh, Wawita! Wawita mia!
I carry you in my manta,
braiding you into my hair.

Listen to what I say:
Those who in confusion
decorate walls with my messages,
I see
cluelessly dismissing your efforts
to use the fragments of our wisdom,
forged in the moisture of our conquered lands.

Oh, hijita mia!
I know why you cry.
I've tasted the blood of your blood and the dirt under the boots
of forebears to whom you stand tall.
But tangled my braids are not.

Remember who you are.
Maintain the cycle.
Tend the fire.
Weave the rhythm of time.
Harvest the wisdom that is yours.
When young pioneers question your truth,
let the callus of our reality open their eyes,
and together, find harmony to roar."

A powerful and important aspect of moving beyond internalized domination and embracing our full selves is reconciling with our lineage and with the parts of ourselves that we may have hidden or buried due to shame or cultural expectations. In my early years of living in the US, I didn't want to be recognized as Latina, because I'd witnessed the experiences of women who looked like me. I feared that I'd miss out on several opportunities. I had internalized these notions from my own observations of the grading system that existed within the social landscape of my new environment. Not to mention, I'd experienced my share of "othering" treatment, as well as experiences of people looking down on me due to my accent or my cinnamon-brown skin. In so many ways, I used various aspects of my identity to camouflage my suffering. For me, identity was a manta woven from only the best and most curated threads. I only felt Peruvian when someone had something good to say about my birthplace.

Something changed when I led my first spiritual retreat in Perú. I began to see how disconnected and dismembered I was. Although I was in one of the most mystically spirited territories in the world, I was having a challenging time. Many memories from my childhood surfaced in ways that felt painful and unwanted. Nothing seemed to be helping to soothe my pain. I also noticed the irony of being a Peruvian who was hosting retreats primarily to foreigners to Perú but didn't want to have anything to do with Peruvians themselves.

At the retreat center where I was staying, I saw a beautiful *colibrí*, or hummingbird, which reminded me that my abuelita used to say these birds are sacred and only appear when the Divine is ready to talk to us and we are ready to hear the messages. I was in the midst of debilitating grief amid my attempts to hold a container for over a dozen retreat participants. As I walked the grounds of the retreat center in the Sacred Valley, though, I opened my sentipensante to that hummingbird.

Many years later, I realized and clearly saw that the place where I was staying was located on the slopes of the mountain that would become my *Apu*. In Pacha philosophy, an Apu is a custodial force of Nature that rules over the specific terrain in which one is born or where one is spiritually connected. In fact, I would later learn that my spiritual maestro, Amaru, called this mountain *Taita* (Quechua for "father"). Even though I wouldn't meet him until years later, it was synchronistic that I had chosen a retreat center in an area that would prove to be such an important place in my own spiritual pilgrimage.

As I looked around at the majestic mountains, I came to understand that they were not merely rocks rising from the earth. They were alive and a manifestation of the Divine. During the retreat, I began to ask myself deeper, uncomfortable questions that eventually led to a spiritual reconciliation with myself, my ancestors, and my connection to the Creator. I also realized after that vivid experience that it was time to reorient. The process of being able to see into the spiritual realm guided me to acknowledge and accept my gifts; the door to understanding had opened, and I was being called to accept the capacity to see beyond what the human eye can see.

I also began to recognize that it was time to stop mixing so many spiritual modalities, as it was keeping the energy—which can be seen as its own being—from doing what it was intended to. It was almost as if the energy were confused about the direction in which to move. My abuelita had told me not to mix different systems of primordial forces by taking a bunch of components or codes from different traditions and putting them together into one giant manta full of disjointed and disarrayed threads. Elders often remind us to be cautious about this because not only is it disrespectful, it can also be dangerous. The whispers from my lineage continued to come to me. Although other philosophies and medicinal practices had been valuable and had shown me ways to connect with different energetic and mystical pathways, my ancestors supported me in remembering the way I was meant to do this work.

In this chapter, we will continue the journey of healing by weaving our own remedies for our wounds based on our connection with our ancestors and elders. It can be deeply inspiring to work with a variety of traditions—but it is even more therapeutic to reconcile with the traditions of our own ancestors and to weave ourselves back into the manta of our lineage.

EXPANDING AWARENESS OF CULTURAL INSENSITIVITY

Many people seem to be called to traditions outside of their family lineage. Sometimes, this may point to the possibility that they actually have ancestors in other places, which is something that we are learning more about with the rise of DNA testing. However, it can be concerning if we are using a tradition outside of our lineage to avoid doing the emotional and spiritual labor of getting to know our own ancestors. This can be another form of spiritual bypassing that causes disconnection and leads to the adoption of a colonizing mentality.

Thankfully, even if we have been re-planted many times over, we can always connect with the winds that scattered our seed and follow their melody back to the places where our ancestors long for us to return and to make what was broken whole again.

I continue to regard embodiment practices from South Asia as a sacred medicine, although my relationship to them now is different. In keeping with the medicine analogy, it's important to note that just as we're not supposed to take antibiotics our entire life, it is the same with the medicine we access—it is meant to bring us into homeostasis so that we feel more rooted in who we are. When I felt I had achieved enough of a sense of equilibrium, I began to ask new questions. For example, even though I might not have felt like I was appropriating it, how did I feel about the philosophical system of yoga, nurtured by the people of India and South Asia for so long, being primarily represented by people who didn't come out of that culture . . . but who were the ones reaping its rewards?

Numerous people who access these kinds of medicines will often affirm that they have the duty to heal other people with the very thing that healed them. However, it is crucial to ask, "Is this really my place?"

Unfortunately, being outside the culture that brought these mighty remedies into the world, usually over a long period of time, can set us up to replicate exploitation. When people take on a blended style and remove practices from their cultural context, it can get very convoluted. This was something I recognized after holding a spiritual retreat in Cusco, Perú, a place of healing rooted in its own rich cultural traditions and ancestral practices. I began to consider that by bringing medicine from a completely different culture into this land, I was removing the autonomy of the people who lived here to provide healing through their own traditions and practices. I was also limiting my capacity to experience healing directly through my own lineage.

Here, it's essential to recognize that there are various forms of lineage. There is blood lineage, which refers to the heritage and ancestry connected to our DNA, as well as the multilayered codes we inherit from the people in this lineage. In addition, many of us feel that we are connected to a spiritual lineage, which encompasses the wisdom traditions that pass down from teachers to students, although there may not be shared bonds of race, ethnicity, cultural customs, etc.

There is also cultural lineage, which refers to the structures and rituals of the culture in which we and our family are situated, maybe re-planted. For people who might come in through spiritual lineage, they can also inherit a sense of cultural lineage to that place, because they become proximate to that particular community. Ideally, they are connected to the heartache and pain of that community, especially if they are immersed in sacred reciprocity. Of course, this doesn't always happen, especially if someone who comes from outside the community attempts to come into it with the desire to "save" the people within it or be a leader over it.

The general expectation is that such a person is humble enough to become part of the community but the community has no obligation to become one of them.

Even when we feel a sense of connection to a spiritual lineage, we have to be careful about overharvesting practices we do not share a blood or cultural lineage with. In general, within Andean society, you either receive lineage through blood relations and proximity to the actual community, usually via marriage, as well as through the communal codes that signal a sense of shared culture. However, the lineage through which many people are coming to Andean spirituality today is the spiritual one.

Unfortunately, there are no easy protocols to deal with this. There is no appointed representative of Andean religion such as a Pope or Dalai Lama, so there isn't a definitive process through which outsiders can systematically access information in the most sustainable way. Although Andean religion and spirituality has a structure, the practices vary depending on the community as well as what the elders pass on. Many foreigners flock to these Andean teachings, and over the past several decades, many of them have presented themselves as "authentic" lineage holders. This confers a sense of authority on people who may not be rooted in the culture and everyday concerns of the Andean people. But even if they believe they are, internalized domination can create schisms in the sense of relationship to the land and the people who live there.

It is critical that those of us curious about spirituality exercise responsibility and discernment when it comes to asking ourselves whether we are perpetuating internalized domination and a colonizer mentality of appropriation that either weakens teachings or fractures them from their cultural context. This is important when we are looking at sacred Andean and other Indigenous traditions, where the people within those cultures are in a process of reclaiming and reconciling with their own spiritual birthrights, which have been fragmented and abused for hundreds of years. If they are next of kin to their traditions, it is essential that they be the lineage holders.

It is up to everyone to exercise the discernment that's necessary to access the medicine they need; however, the path to becoming whole starts when we reconcile with our own lineages. This starts with the conviction that we are all related, and that ancestral knowledge, at its core, has communal threads that are linked to Nature. All of us can come back to these basic roots. We can recognize that Nature is our primary healer and teacher who provides the most elaborate and precise methods, while also noting that there is often a danger of overharvesting the practices of people who have already been dispossessed.

For example, many people travel to Perú to partake in Ayahuasca ceremonies because they believe this medicine has the potential to heal them. This might be true, but the problem is often connected to the approach. If we are treating Ayahuasca as an object that is ours to take for our own enrichment, this is another form of spiritual consumerism. Also, within these sacred traditions, there are many plant medicines that were meant to be kept in secret, small batches. The demand for this type of medicine today is devastating—socially, culturally, and ecologically—and it is shaking the roots of Indigenous communities. As foreigners seek out individual healing, conveniently self-appointed "shamans" have cropped up to meet the demand, compromising the integrity of the rituals and adapting age-old customs to cater to those with the money to pay for it. We cannot look at the global demand for plant medicine without recognizing that the heirs to this knowledge have often been pushed aside or have succumbed to the plant-medicine craze in order to gain influence and wealth. If we cannot implement sustainable ways to grow together as human beings in relationship to Nature and one another, this approach will always lead to harmful and disrespectful ways of pursuing our individual over our collective healing.

Certainly, I've heard the justification for using plant medicine from Westerners, who might say, "Well, if it's from Nature, nobody owns it, so this isn't appropriation." While the roots, herbs, and fruits come from Nature, they have also been treated, cared for, and stewarded by the ancestors and guardians of those lands. These plant medicines resisted eradication with the help of their ancestors. Specific codes have been developed over many hundreds, even thousands, of years, in collaboration between the people and Nature. The grandchildren of those guardians are connected to the medicine, just as they are connected to the wounds and hardships that were endured in the struggle to protect it. That lineage cannot be separated from the medicine itself. When outsiders access these medicines, they weave themselves into the ancestral memory of the trauma and challenges incurred in the resistance of annihilation. The nuna that transformed this medicine is the birthright of the people who have lovingly cultivated it, which can't be undermined.

Of course, I am not suggesting that the plant medicine of the Andes and the Amazon be kept only for their people only. This would break the codes of Pacha philosophy, which is about harmonious inclusivity. However, I believe that it's our responsibility to safely contain this sacred knowledge so it isn't propagated from a purely Western-centric viewpoint—one that "molds" the teachings to cater to a Western perspective and context. Integration is necessary so we can all contribute to a world of genuine respect and shared influence. According to Andean prophecy, those of us from *la tierra viva* have the heart to awaken the hearts of others, but we all are called to weave connections between the four cardinal points that exist on this planet.

This is why I encourage those who may be seeking spiritual medicine to consider that which comes from their own blood lineage. The more you tune in, the more you might sense the longing for the land and untold stories of your ancestors calling you. You might sense the smell of the land and hear its voice, even if you have been re-planted elsewhere. These are your roots and your blood and your body, asking you to pay attention.

RECONCILING WITH WHERE WE ARE FROM

Our ancestral roots are inextricable from the land, and some part of our nuna will always be in relationship with it. When I talk about the importance of reconnecting with our roots, I am not suggesting that there aren't other important aspects of the healing pilgrimage. However, our ancestral lineage is an important resource when it comes to finding a sense of harmony, balance, belonging, safety, and connection. Many of us have been uprooted and re-planted, and we are contending with so many unaddressed wounds—which then get replicated in our fragmented, lonely societies. When we are missing an elemental connection to the land, we also are missing connection to ourselves and to one another. In addition, we carry our ancestors in our own blood and bones, even when we don't consciously realize this. We carry their wisdom and their wounds, as well as their songs, metaphors, and stories; when we do the important work of reconciling with them, we contribute to healing not just ourselves, but also generations to come. We experience a greater sense of ease and joy in our sentipensante, and this is reflected in our relationships and the communities we weave together.

As we discussed in chapters 1 and 2, many of us have struggled with feeling disconnected from a sense of grounding within a supportive culture that steers us to be a part of a larger fabric. Many of us don't even know where we are from, as the threads of our family's manta have been frayed by trauma, negligence, or the simple business of survival.

Beloved friend, if you have picked up this book, it's likely that you are the needle that may very well be responsible for threading that manta back together and mending the holes with your care. After all, in order for the manta to exist, someone needs to be there to weave it. And even if we don't know where to start, the mere act of beginning to question where we come from and to tap into the cultural traditions and therapeutic methods of our ancestors is a huge step we can take.

However, it's good to be aware and to exercise unapologetic truth and mature intervention. We must also recognize if we might be "picking and choosing" which ancestors to work with. My mixed-race client, Lulu, came to me for guidance on how to pay tribute to her family's history. Her mom had mostly raised her, while her dad was largely absent, working to pay bills. Thus, he was emotionally unavailable to the family. Her mother's side of the family represented to her a sense of protection and passion, while her father's side was marked by duty and the expectation of attaining social and financial stability. So, when she came to me, she mostly wanted to focus on her mother's side of the family.

I explained to her that it's not about picking and choosing which side to honor when it comes to acknowledging our ancestors and addressing intergenerational wounds. There's a difference between not knowing one side of our family's history and purposely neglecting it. But dismissing one side means that we miss out on a crucial part of the healing and reconciliation process with our ancestors.

As noted earlier, Pacha philosophy believes in the principle of Sumaq Kawsay, which teaches us that every object or phenomenon can be understood by analyzing its two interdependent opposites. Just as the night cannot exist without day, our spiritual DNA is a fusion of both sides of our family. We cannot simply ignore what we don't like. So, it's on us to determine when it's the right time to embark on connecting with all parts of our heritage, who we are, and where we come from.

"I get it," Lulu said, "but is it okay for me to start with my mother's side before I move on to my dad's?"

"Of course!" I responded. "In fact, that might give you a stronger basis from which to start exploring your father's side. Just be sure you aren't neglecting it altogether."

As someone with roots in both the Catholic Church and Indigenous Andean traditions, I have also recognized the potency of not choosing one side of our family, heritage, or religion over any of the others. This can expand our methods of healing as we come into a more authentic relationship with our unique background, one that embraces complexity without seeing the forest for the trees. For example, in Perú, the Catholic Church retains components of ancestral practices, such as respect for the symbolic resonance of the sun and moon, so it can be impactful and liberating to honor the syncretic weaving together of different traditions of our ancestry. Connecting with our roots is not about clinging to any false ideas about purity and deserving grace. Rather, it is about gathering the aspects that guide us to step into our wholeness without shame, and with the willingness to claim our complexity and sovereignty.

By our first consultation, Lulu decided that she would be working with her mother's side of the family, but she shared that she felt disconnected from her family's traditions surrounding life and death. However, together, we explored what it would mean to learn more about the tradition of El Día de los Muertos. At first, Lulu was reluctant because she felt that it had become overly commercialized, especially in the Western world. Lulu had been studying Tibetan Buddhist traditions around how to honor the dead and their transition to the next life, but she'd never felt a close connection to the two-day holiday reuniting the dead and living that so many of her own family members revered. "It feels like a cliché," Lulu said at first, when I suggested that she build an altar and prepare foods for the dead in the way her own family did.

However, instead of simply adopting external traditions because she felt uncomfortable approaching her own family's traditions, I suggested to Lulu that she do the emotional and spiritual labor of recognizing the time-honored ways in which her ancestors had come to revere the connections between the living and the dead—no matter how "commercial" or trendy they'd become. For Lulu, it was a profound journey that helped her to grow in sweetness, compassion, and introspection—and that also prepared her to work with her paternal lineage.

Many of us who are of mixed ancestry, just like me and Lulu, will find it easiest to start with the side that we are most proximate to, generationally and spiritually. Many of us will feel a distinct calling to one aspect of our lineage. But again, it's essential to be aware that we aren't focusing on one side in order to avoid the other(s), because eventually we will have to reconcile with all of them.

If you are someone who doesn't have many details about your heritage, please know that you're not alone. It's possible that you are adopted or separated from your family of origin. Perhaps you come from a multitude of cultural backgrounds. Maybe you and your family assimilated into the dominant culture. Perhaps you come from an Indigenous tradition or are a descendant of enslaved people who were forcefully wrested away from their lands and traditions. Whatever the case, it's possible to begin exactly as and where you are. Even if we don't know their names, the voices of our grandmothers and grandfathers from many generations ago are still lovingly whispering to us, beckoning us home.

However, even in the places where we are limited by our knowledge of our forebears, we can connect with the everlasting reality: Nature is our ancestor. The water that runs through our body belongs to the ocean. The bones that hold us up are connected to the minerals in the Earth. The skin that covers us is made of primordial stardust. So, even if we do not have the benefit of immediate stories from our family lineage, the story of Nature and the multiverse lives in our DNA.

My sincere and loving invitation is that you reflect on your own journey of learning to embrace your family story, traditions, and medicine. Can you embrace the emotional labor of ancestral work for a more faithful connection to your heritage? The path is yours to forge, and I encourage you to embark on it with respect, depth, and authenticity.

MIRROR THE JAGUAR
The Medicines from Which You Benefit

- Take time to do some primal journaling about the various forms of medicine that you've discovered on your own healing and spiritual pilgrimage. Consider the various phases in your life when you sought healing. To whom and what did you turn? Be very specific about the cultural traditions, even if they may not seem obvious at first glance, and the actual teachers from whom you learned.

- For each medicine you've identified, answer the following questions:
    - Why did you need it at the time? What was the result you were hoping to get?
    - What did you wish to gain? I encourage you to dig deep. For example, did you desire a sense of glory? Were you escaping something in your life that was painful? Did you feel disconnected from your roots, and you simply wanted to feel connected to something?
    - How did you incorporate it into your life? Were you diligent about learning about the culture from which it came, and the people who lovingly stewarded it?

- How did these medicines help you?
- Is there any possibility that you may have inadvertently overharvested the medicines in ways that perpetuated further harm? Why or why not?
- What are the spiritual medicines from your own blood and cultural lineage that you're curious about? Have you explored them yet? Why or why not?
- In what ways can you begin the process of reconciling with your own lineage through exploring its wisdom traditions and healing practices? Write down at least three ways.

RECLAIMING LANGUAGE

Language is a profound aspect of reconnecting with our lineage and healing the wounds of the past, which continue to live through us. This is especially true if we stop to really think about some of the spiritual jargon that we indiscriminately apply. I once asked my maestro Amaru, "What does it mean to you when people call you a shaman? How do you feel about that?"

He laughed. "I'm not a shaman, I'm a *sacerdote* (priest)!" he replied.

This made me feel sad, as I recognize that the term *shaman* has been misallocated and misused. It is derived from the Manchu-Tungus word *šamán*, which translates to "one who knows" and applies to the very specific spiritual practices of a very specific group of people. Now, it is widely used to refer to people from a variety of spiritual traditions and bodies of knowledge based in Nature. But language has its own nuna and carries potent wisdom—especially with respect to the blood of those who defended it against eradication. If outsiders to a tradition are using it in an "authoritative" way to declare their embryonic understanding about that tradition and its cultural symbolism, language becomes another tool of colonization that removes autonomy from the people within these traditions.

Sadly, many people unwittingly apply terms like *shaman* to themselves and others, without fully considering that language carries heritage memory, and meaning and vibrations get fragmented when a word is removed from its context. Instead of assuming that those working with the elements of Nature and ancestral medicines are shamans, we can make it a healthy habit to ask teachers or elders for the name that accurately conveys what they embody.

For example, when I hear people use the term *Pachamama* out of context, it pains me. This overharvested term is often translated to refer to an earth goddess, but this is a narrow perspective. Pachamama is a force of fertility and sustenance and the conjunction of all the elements, directions, and stratas of life. When we take it out of context to fit it into linear narratives, we risk losing its sacred meaning. The closest translation is that Pachamama is "a place or a land that is deeply blessed, that engenders and breeds life, that is Nature itself." All humans are Pachamama. However, it continues to be overused and decontextualized, and I do not wish to perpetuate its abuse.

Also, Pachamama is a Quechua word, and for generations, this language was frowned upon in Perúvian society, as it connoted lower status. At one point in our history, speaking it was practically illegal. Thus, hearing Quechua words from people who have no idea what my ancestors had to endure to ensure the survival of this sacred tongue causes the intergenerational wound within me to bleed. In fact, my process of reconciliation with the Quechua language gives it a different weight when I hear its words spoken in the Western world.

I grew up knowing that Quechua was the language of the people who were servants in urban areas like Lima. I was inculcated into believing that Quechua was inferior to the Spanish used by people with lighter skin and more education, not realizing that I had been denied access to the majestic cultural legacy and way of seeing the world that comes from knowing the language of my ancestors. I went through the humbling process of learning Quechua at the age of forty, and today, I use Quechua terms with tender, profound respect. With my utmost effort and conviction, I try not to misuse them. I decided to learn Quechua in order to claim the birthright of my birthplace's history and traditions. This was a debt I owed to the abuelitas of my abuelitas. Today, in the

Andean territories that comprise several countries, including Perú, there are approximately ten million Quechua speakers—plus me. I intend to be a steward who will work to keep the legacy of my ancestors alive.

Beloved friend, it's possible that you, like many others who have been re-planted in different places or who have lost a sense of connection to ancestral ways, have also lost your connection to an ancestral language. Many other Mestizo people only have access to Spanish but not the languages of their Indigenous roots, which cuts them off from a powerful link to their own spiritual DNA. But this is also true for others. Often, in the Western world, assimilation into the dominant culture means that ancestral languages are quickly lost, sometimes within a generation. Many of my own clients have told me stories about how they come from families where people are bilingual or trilingual but that they either lost their "mother tongue" when they began going to school, or their parents didn't teach it to them because they believed that speaking only English would ensure their success. These examples don't even include the violent consequences of colonization, where many people from cultures around the world, especially Indigenous ones, were forced to give up their languages and traditions altogether.

If this is familiar to you, please know that you're not alone. It's possible for you to reconnect with your ancestral language(s) if you choose, which can be an impactful bridge to the culture and traditions of your forebears. Language, as a construct of the thinking mind, is a paradigm of making meaning and experiencing belonging, and it's a potent aspect of cultural recovery.

Aside from beginning to learn your own ancestral language(s), you can also be an advocate and encourage the young people in your life to recuperate wisdom and tradition in the same way. Moreover, if you are enticed to work with the medicine of a tradition that is not in your blood lineage, be intentional as to whether you are parroting the sacred chants and prayers of these traditions. Please know that for many traditions, sacred prayers have been kept and maintained in a state of secrecy, especially when they contended with the forces of domination. It is a great privilege to work with this kind of material, especially because people may have paid for speaking these languages with their very lives.

When I began learning Quechua, I began to recognize that it is our responsibility not to glamorize sacred words from other languages, through mispronunciation, cultural decontextualization, or simply working with bad information that removes these terms from their actual meaning. If you're working with a dead language, ask why it's a dead language. Be respectful. This may require speaking with the people who are custodians of the language and asking for permission to use the prayers, or specific guidance on how to do so in a way that is honoring. Often, as in Quechua, these words have multiple meanings rather than a simple interpretation, so it's important to listen and vulnerably receive the meaning with your full sentipensante.

I encourage you to continue your own healing process by diligently researching the languages that your ancestors spoke, that were woven through the sacred and mundane rituals of their own lives. I encourage you to reclaim your own birthright and to be the steward who continues to thread the needle and ensure that the manta of your mother tongue is continually renewed.

RECONCILING WITH THE LAND

We have talked a lot about Nature and the importance of connecting to the land and the elements, so this chapter would be incomplete without speaking to how our attempts to reconcile with our own lineage must necessarily welcome a connection with the land.

I often find that, while people might feel a sense of disconnection from the land of the place where they live (whether it's their birthplace or not), we are all often compelled to "find ourselves" by traveling around the world to touristy sacred sites that are outside of our ancestry lineage. My question is: Why not start exactly where you are? Also, why not reconnect to the land and your ancestors, even if you've been re-planted elsewhere?

My experience is that when we visit the land of our ancestors, healing can occur almost instantly. For example, one of my clients, Sara, had been a nomad for years—moving from place to place without feeling she belonged anywhere. When she shared a desire to heal her roots and find "my place," I suggested that she make a pilgrimage to a location that was special to her ancestors. Sara learned about the farm where her grandparents and great-grandparents lived. One day, she visited this farm, which had passed into the hands of a new owner long ago, with her children. She told the person who had taken over, "My grandmother used to live here, and there's a tree that she used to play in. Is it possible for us to see it?" The owner said yes, and when Sara visited the tree and made a simple sacred contract with it, her life began to transform. She found a greater sense of community and belonging in the place where she was currently living, such that she no longer felt the itch to keep changing locations. She had moved through the process of re-planting herself in her current environment, by communing with the tree that her grandmother had loved so much—as well as making a sacred contract to ask permission of the land where she now lived.

As I often tell my clients, we may face the world as one person, but we come into this world with thousands at our back and in our hearts. These are our ancestors, and they are deeply intertwined with the land.

But in addition to connecting with the land of our ancestors, we must connect with the land where we have been re-planted. Beginning with the knowledge that we are all in relationship with everything, including Nature, we can hold the awareness that every region has its own sacred places—such as rivers, forests, mountains, and beaches. In the land where we live, we can pay respect to these mighty guardians and ask for permission to re-plant ourselves and our offspring. We can ask for the ability to be responsible stewards of the land, acknowledging all that it has lived through and hosted, including the original stewards.

The language of communication we use will depend on where we are from, as well as the codes we use to communicate with Nature and the spiritual realm. For some, an intricate sacred contract invoking the ancestors of the land will feel necessary; for others, a simple prayer to the Divine will suffice. Whatever we choose, our intention and sincere desire must be to re-plant ourselves in connection with the land, working with the sacred guardians in service of the entire community.

This will allow us to not perpetuate the contemporary Western connection to land, which is all about ownership and meeting our own individual needs rather than those of the larger community of humans and non-humans.

Learning the codes of a place isn't purely about using your own intuition. You can also educate yourself about what the original stewards of the land may have done, and what their relationship to the land was. For example, one of my clients re-planted to the Washington, DC area with her family but found that she was struggling to integrate with the unique social demands of her new environment and community. Her children especially found it difficult to make friends at school and participate in the new culture.

I asked my client what kinds of outdoor activities she and her children enjoyed. They were all interested in kayaking, so I suggested kayaking as an entry point to learning about the significance of the Potomac River, which the people of the Chesapeake region heavily relied on as a trade route. When my client and her children rented a kayak and navigated the river with reverence and gratitude, they started feeling more connected to the people around them. They also developed a deeper appreciation for the natural world and the original stewards of these areas—especially the river that was their primary source of food and a vital transportation route across the seasons.

It is important to remember that building relationships and learning the codes of the Indigenous custodians of the land, who may now be spread across the region due to colonization, is our sacred duty as re-planted people. And, in the case of my client, carrying out this sacred duty gave her a greater understanding and appreciation of her new community. Of course, it can be complicated in places like Perú, where many groups of people may have stewarded the land, from pre-Columbian to pre-pre-Columbian. We must use our own discernment, but in general, you can follow the codes of the civilization that preceded the one you are in now. Of course, this requires context and awareness of the type of connection they had to the land.

There is no end to how we can directly work with the lands of our ancestors, as well as those where we have been re-planted. I even make it a practice to ask different lands—the place where I live, as well as places to which my ancestors belong—to speak to one another. This facilitates the healing and repair work that may need to be done in our lineage, especially with respect to intergenerational and cultural wounds.

Working directly with the land is a way to weave ourselves back into the manta of belonging. Healing our connection to lineage can always be supported by a genuine desire to build a reciprocal relationship with Nature. Nature itself is the force that embraces all of life and that weaves all beings together in the manta of interdependence. When we build a healthy relationship to the land—one that is respectful, historically aware, and connected to the complex ecology of a place—we come to realize that we are never alone. We also come to see ourselves as inherently worthy and as being holders of grace—complementary expressions of the same living, collective, and cyclical being: Earth.

EMBODY THE JAGUAR

Becoming a Good Ancestor

Journal and reflect on the following:

- Who were your ancestors, and what is your relationship to them? That is, do you feel any connection to them? Do you know who they were? Even if they lived long ago, do you have a sense of their stories, as well as their strengths and weaknesses?
- What kind of ancestor do you want to be? What are your strengths and weaknesses?
- How can you connect with the lands of your ancestors and the lands where you've been re-planted?

Craft a sacred contract for yourself, using your answers to these questions. Perhaps a sacred contract includes making regular pilgrimages to the land(s) of your ancestors and finding ways to be of service to the people who still live there. Considering our own responsibility to future generations requires that we continue to unpack our own family traditions and do the impactful work of healing and reconciling with our roots.

Please know that this is work that will be supported by the KARE method, but it can be very uncomfortable to dive into. Just as you have done the work of understanding and working through your personal wounds (which is, for many people, an ongoing endeavor), the work of understanding and working through ancestral wounds requires unapologetic truth and mature intervention.

Reconciling with your blood ancestors doesn't mean you accept and justify everything they have done. It just means that you are now willing to turn your sentipensante toward your own roots, which are a part of your medicine—even if you have not seen it that way in the past.

8

WORKING WITH ELDERS AND WISDOM KEEPERS

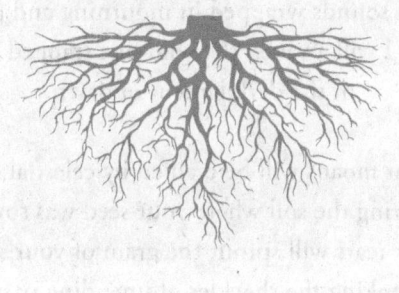

Within My Waters

Allow me to be your mirror, hermana mía.
May you see in the pupils of my eyes
the grandeur of your volcano, full of heat.

With gentle presence,
I will receive your weary heart
and slink through the labyrinth of your being,
finding your light projected from the stars.

Through sounds wrapped in mourning and pleasure,
I will awaken the wild one trapped
in the dark lament of dawn.

Your silent moans will be cradled by celestial melodies,
stirring the soil where your seed was sown.
Your tears will sprout the grain of your soul,
breaking the shackles of unending pasts.

Your roots will remember the way to the sun,
intertwining with the wisdom of your grandmothers,
who await your return, dressed in multicolored trees.

With each step toward sovereignty,
your sacred waters will accompany you,
transforming your essence into rivers of moonlight.

The stones will speak of your power,
watching a bird with broken wings
heal from your waterfall,
ready to soar once more.

In my intimate talks with the fire, I speak of your triumphs
and I bow to my winds that brought you to my waters,
where I will lovingly keep you.

Beloved friend, I want you to pause and feel the strength of the jaguar that has been your constant companion along this journey. The jaguar has been a profound and powerful teacher for me and so many others, but I want to reiterate that teachers are all around us. Nature is a teacher whose multiplicity means that we have the power to learn from everything around us, which is always talking. Our own nuna is a wonderful teacher too, but the journey of reconciliation and calling our nuna back always requires conscious guidance. Life is our teacher, but teachers in human, embodied form are also necessary along the path.

I've heard the question many times: "Do we really need teachers on the spiritual path?" We do! This type of work is not meant to be done alone. Of course, our teachers might offer us knowledge, but it is our job to integrate it! It's wonderful when we begin our investigation in the sacred vessel of our sentipensante—where we might ascertain what appeals to us, and where we feel driven to explore further—but in order to expand beyond our limited or programmed ideas shaping our existence, we need guidance and direction. We need a faithful mirror who can reflect back to us the depths of our grace and wholeness, which we may not be able to see or sense. It's also important to remember that we are all in some way mirrors for one another.

It can be dangerous to walk the path of reconciliation alone because it's easy to lose our perceptions of reality and get stuck in a world or realm that is not of the living. I have encountered many individuals in the roles of "teachers" who insist that they don't need the guidance of a teacher or mentor because they are communicating directly with the spirit realm. As we'll explore, there are many signs we can look to that will ensure we, as well as the teachers we might be learning from, are walking a path of integrity and that we are not merely kidding ourselves or consorting with influences that ultimately aren't good for us.

The experience of teaching and stewardship exists in a much more transactional way in our modern world, which is why it's important to be discerning when working with a teacher. Because we live in a world with wounds related to internalized dominance, it's important to remember that our human teachers are not absolved of the human experience; they are humans, with their own gifts, talents, blind spots, and areas of growth. We must be realistic about what they can teach us. We can benefit from their wisdom, but there may also be limits to their capacity. For example, if you are a person from a non-Western country who wants to reconcile with some of the traditions within your blood lineage, yet you are working with a teacher of European descent who is further removed from the challenges you are facing—which go beyond purely spiritual considerations—this doesn't mean your teacher doesn't have wisdom to share. They might be capable of holding space for you, but you may find that it's necessary to work with someone whose experiences can support the fullness and complexity of your personal path.

I encourage you to beware of hierarchical models that impose a fixed student/teacher relationship where the teacher is always in a position of power over the student, as well as teachers who are not modest enough to allow themselves to be lifelong students. It's important to work with teachers who have integrity and are not merely using their position to overpower students or to perpetuate domination.

Beloved friend, I invite you to continue to attune to the signs all around you so that you can receive the teachings of Nature, which are always freely given but are often overlooked or misinterpreted. Of course, a human, embodied teacher is one of the most impactful ways to learn and become fluent in the language of Nature. The key is exercising discernment in all your interactions, so that you might receive a clear reflection from the world around you that serves to lead you back to yourself.

MY PATH TO AMARU

Over twenty-five years of spiritual inquiry, curiosity, and investigation, I've encountered countless teachers—from professors, to coaches, to mentors, and everyone in between. However, there are only a few I consider to be my *teachers*. These people are dear to my sentipensante. In these relationships, I experience friendship, respect, and reciprocity. My contribution and inquiries are not an inconvenience to them, but a way in which they can also learn something new. It was in this context that I met Amaru.

After the retreat that I led in Perú, I received the calling of my nuna from all directions, and I started looking for answers. As with other moments in my life, I started out on my own, reading many different texts and questioning those readings. I spent hours researching the Andean cosmovision and Pacha religion. I started documenting information about my family from both sides, questioning why we'd persisted with certain traditions for generations. Some of the stories I collected were broken; some were mystified and glorified; others were raw and painful to confront. But all of these stories were important in helping me to make sense of the life I was living.

I knew that I had to process my discoveries about my ancestry in a brand-new way. And I knew that my current teachers and their specific lineages would not be able to assist me with this in the way that I needed. I also recognized that texts could only take me so far; I needed an embodied experience of exploring my roots. There is a Spanish phrase, *la sangre llama*, which refers to the call of our own blood. That call was becoming louder and louder, and it was time for me to answer it.

The next step in my process of rediscovering harmony was to learn from others, so I signed up to receive classes and seminars from renowned maestros and scholars of Andean traditions. They all hailed from various territories and countries, and to my surprise and dismay, in some of the spiritual teachings, I recognized aspects I'd already encountered in the overarching "new age" movement. While some of the teachers certainly conducted themselves with integrity, a startling number appeared to be using the knowledge for personal gain—such as material wealth, or the admiration of the general public. This made me pause, especially given everything I was learning about the legacy of domination that hung like a storm cloud over the Andean people. I also noticed that some of what I was hearing from these teachers felt contrary to what I'd learned from my own deep dive into Pacha philosophy. I recognized that because many of their students were of European descent, they were adapting the teachings to fit their expectations of what these students could digest. On top of all this, they were usually charging small fortunes for knowledge that, in some cases, wasn't even theirs to share.

I met Amaru at a seminar with an organization in Perú that supports Peruvians to recuperate ancestral wisdom. Amaru's wisdom immediately made sense to me. Some part of me instinctively knew that I should connect with him further. I asked him if he'd be willing to support my journey, and he graciously said yes.

Years have passed since my first encounter with him. Amaru has led me through multiple sacred contracts. We've logged countless hours of conversations. I've made multiple pilgrimages to his Apu in la Sierra del Perú. Now, through his recommendation and introduction, his Apu has welcomed me and then became my benefactor. In many ways, although there are certainly meaningful boundaries that keep our relationship as maestro and student sacred, he has opened up his home to me as if I was his sister. He also knows every member of my family and inner circle by name, as we usually call their nuna into our sacred-contract work and request their wholeness, grace, and harmony—including those in the unseen realms. We have worked together on projects in his community in the same way that we often work together on projects that impact my community in the place where I am re-planted. Amaru constantly reminds me of the principles of Sumaq Kawsay—namely, that we are all in relationship with one another. My relationship with Amaru is one of profound mutual trust, respect, care, and solidarity—not only for us as individuals but for the collective.

FINDING THE RIGHT TEACHER FOR YOU

I've learned a lot from Amaru about what it takes to be a truly remarkable teacher. In fact, working alongside him has guided me to cultivate my own medicine and share it with others. First and foremost, I believe that a good teacher has integrity. They live by example and embody their message. They do not pretend to be something they aren't. They are able to maintain a sense of humor about their humanity and limitations. At the same time, they don't use "I'm only human" as an excuse for misconduct or abusive behavior. They act with consistency. And in their communities, people come to them for practical wisdom on how to live life with a sense of congruence and integrity because they embody such qualities.

Of course, there is certainly no single way to teach. Teaching styles and proclivities are as varied as the sizes of the rainbows of earthly existence. I am grateful to each of my teachers who have guided me in the many disciplines and subjects I have studied. Some of them took interest in me, some of them remained at a distance, and some of them didn't even know me. However, because I have an extremely curious mind and heart, and because I flourish in relationships that include opportunities for dialogue, it was important for me to form close bonds with my teachers. It took me several years to fully understand this. Early in my spiritual pilgrimage and discovery of the meaning of life, I was still getting to know the hows and whys of embodying Lorena!

Unfortunately, many people who find themselves on a similar path struggle with trusting people. They might feel insecure or inferior due to past wounding, which can put them at a disadvantage when it comes to establishing sustainable relationships with teachers. I remember one of my clients telling me that she feared approaching teachers, especially those who embody intellectual knowledge, because she worried that she'd be "pestering" them with her inquiries. A young and tender part of her was concerned they wouldn't have time for her, especially because they are so "important." I told her that I'd long ago come to the conclusion that the old adage "When the student is ready, the teacher will appear" was true. In some ways, the time we take to approach teachers can serve us well. We can prioritize our own inner work and rely on our resources, based on what we've learned over the years.

Personally, I continued to do this, even as the right teachers revealed themselves. I learned that while I could benefit from spiritual mentors, it is crucial not to become overly dependent on any one external resource to give me what was my own responsibility to cultivate from within. I also recognized that, with the stable foundation of my own internal guidance system, it was easier to determine the right teachers to work with. In other words, I was not desperate for someone to come along and "teach" me, as I had already done a great deal of the work you've read about and also done throughout this book, especially in the form of the KARE method.

Here are some of the discoveries I made during the process of finding my own teachers, including Amaru.

THEY MIGHT NOT COME IN THE FORM YOU'RE EXPECTING

I learned that it's good to be open to learning from teachers who might be unexpected guides along one's path. We all have our own ideas regarding what we believe we need. I'm sure you probably have your own checklist of prerequisites! For me, my first maestras were my abuelitas, both of whom embodied the gift of healing and who knew how to transmute energy and to embody Pacha, even if it was "unfavorable" to practice within the confines of our culture. When I reconciled with their wisdom and was ready to embody more profound ways of honoring the traditions, I attempted to find a female teacher who embodied the same wisdom as my abuelitas. I made appointments, I reached out, I took classes, and I showed interest in the teachings of female custodians of Andean knowledge. None of these relationships flourished. At some point, I dropped my search, trusting that the right teacher would meet me at the right time.

Although I had imagined that my guide and companion on my pilgrimage would be a woman, due to all the atrocities perpetrated against women in my family over many generations, my winds brought me to

Amaru, who embodies the soft aspect of sweetness and resilience within the Indigenous traditions I was born into. In meeting Amaru, I realized that Pacha always knows best! That is, I needed a masculine presence with nurturing qualities in order to reconcile my own relationship with men, and to also help my female ancestors experience this reconciliation.

Please also remember that a teacher can come to us in a multitude of forms—for example, plants, animals, spirits, ancestors, deities, and even dreams. Nature's ingenuity translates to many opportunities to learn from it. I have personally received meaningful teachings from all kinds of sentient beings, because I recognize that everything has nuna, and everything is alive. The teachable moments in life are innumerable—from conversations with deities or the God of our understanding, to recognition of various animal species' ways of mourning their dead, to the simple laughter and playfulness of small children.

Again, even if we have a sincere desire to commune with a teacher, the paradox is that we often find a teacher when we are not looking for one. I once worked with a client, Karen, who was going through a rough time. She went to Perú, the land of her ancestors, for a personal pilgrimage. She was hoping to find a trusted teacher to reacquaint her with Andean practices, which she'd felt disconnected from for most of her life. However, what she discovered astounded her.

One day, she met an unassuming street vendor who was selling fruit and herbs. Karen was intrigued by this woman, who carried herself with confidence, authority, and a sense of unshakable inner peace. *How can this be?* Karen thought. Her external perception was that this woman had financial hardships and lived a difficult life of needing to peddle her wares in order to make her meager living, which supported several family members. But Karen soon discovered that the woman was a curandera who harbored a great deal of wisdom. Over time, Karen realized that this was the teacher she'd been seeking, so she entered into a more formal apprenticeship with her. The *mamita curandera* (a respectful term for a woman that basically translates to "a mother who heals") explained that she didn't take on many students, only those who were clearly devoted to calling their nuna back. This woman didn't hold retreats or advertise her calling as a maestra—in fact, similar to my own experience with Amaru, it was the curandera's mission to be a teacher to those whose winds brought them to her.

Today, Karen is deeply grateful for her maestra's guidance. "I know that I went to Perú with my own biases and ideas," she says. "I thought my teacher had to look or be a certain way. I thought for sure they'd be teaching at some kind of center, and that they'd be known and celebrated by lots of people. I'm glad I paid attention to that nudge in my heart that led me to get to know my maestra in a deeper way, or else my false ideas might have gotten the best of me!"

Powerful teachers cannot always be found in schools or centers of education and spirituality. They don't necessarily draw huge crowds or fill auditoriums. They might not write books or codify their knowledge for wide consumption. Often, they are rooted in our own communities, doing the same jobs we're doing and living a human experience. And if we enter the spiritual search with biases and egoic ideas about who our teacher should be, we might miss out.

THEY EXERCISE DISCERNMENT IN WHOM THEY CHOOSE TO WORK WITH

Some teachers, especially those who exist within a blood and cultural lineage, are appointed with the responsibility of being wisdom keepers in their respective communities. They are the ones who help to preserve and pass down knowledge. Thus, if we approach such teachers, we must respect that they are the ones who select the how, why, when, and who of passing down their wisdom. Discerning teachers will be able to recognize malicious or misguided intentions on the part of potential students, especially those who might wish to solely take from their knowledge. Such teachers will not be quick to take on students, and if they are, it might be good to ask why! Instead, they will want to know that the student is truly ready, and that their desire to learn is coming from a pure and wholehearted place.

If you are "rejected" by such a teacher, please don't take it personally. Many teachers will willingly take on sincere students, but it's good to recognize that wisdom keepers are rightly concerned about their traditions being overharvested, diluted, or destroyed. For example, some models of teaching, although well-meaning, could result in a transference of knowledge that corrodes the foundation of ancient traditions. If this is the case with a teaching you are interested in receiving, consider that it may be time to seek elsewhere, perhaps within your own family.

THEY WALK IN THE WORLD WITH HUMILITY

It isn't easy to measure humility, but the older I get, the simpler it becomes. For me, it's important that a teacher embody not only knowledge, but also a deep engagement with justice, compassion, and a sense of connection to their communities and the larger world in which they live. They espouse a sense of open-mindedness that is matched by a clear code of ethics. They don't see themselves as being "above" or "better than" others. Rather, they are devoted to lifelong learning in all its forms—not just from books and other recognized teachers, but also from their students, as well as life experiences. The way they treat others—students, people in their inner circle, and others out in the world—often reveals volumes about their character.

We've all seen the stories about spiritual teachers with genuine gifts whose better qualities were taken over by the desire for power. These teachers lose their way and build compounds, usually funded by their followers, and institute rules and regulations that everyone is expected to abide by. In such communities, questions are strongly discouraged, and critical thinking and discernment are not customary. Please, if you encounter a teacher like this, run—don't walk—away. A true teacher knows that they are simply a signpost along the journey, offering good direction as you come home to yourself.

THEY AVOID QUICK FIXES AND CREATING DEPENDENCY

Many spiritual seekers will unknowingly use spirituality to bypass practical considerations, such as treating an illness in a responsible way. As Amaru has constantly told me, Indigenous medicine—such as plant or mineral medicine—doesn't necessarily treat everything, and we must be judicious when it comes to forcing a spiritual solution onto matters that may require a different kind of remedy.

Now, the spiritual realm can absolutely manifest in the physical realm—and when this occurs, spiritual remedies can be useful for us. According to Pacha philosophy, illness is caused by imbalance and disharmony. Sickness is a force with its own nuna, so it needs to eat and be cared for. When we attend to these types of spiritual illnesses, which can manifest in our bodily symptoms, recovery is possible. A good teacher will be able to discern when this is the case, and when it is not—for example, when the imbalance's root cause is more physical.

Likewise, teachers of integrity do not pretend that the remedy you are seeking has a quick fix. Often, it doesn't, especially if there are several root causes that must be attended to. It's like taking a machete and hacking away at the external branches to get to the root. I recall working with a woman who shared a frustrating experience she'd once had with her Andean spiritual teacher. The teacher had asked her to bring a special drink for the sacred contracts they were doing together. Over and over, she came with the wrong drink; over and over, the teacher told her that she had to get this item right in order for the sacred contract to proceed. At first, she was angry. "The ingredients she was asking me for were difficult to gather. I didn't understand why I couldn't use a substitute," she explained.

It turned out that the woman needed to make a special pilgrimage to find the drink her teacher had asked her to prepare. When she finally did, they were able to perform the sacred contract, during which she received many of the answers she had been seeking. Her teacher explained to her that the pilgrimage itself had been an important aspect of the sacred contract. She was constantly in a rush, and she needed to learn that the journey was just as important as the destination, if not more. In fact, the offering of the drink—which she thought was a way to reestablish harmony in her life—ended up being an offering of gratitude and thanksgiving. This, too, was part of the major lesson she'd needed to learn.

Overall, the process took three years. Although she had originally come to her teacher with the desire to quickly heal her emotional and physical problems, she realized in retrospect that she'd gotten exactly what she'd needed, in the perfect amount of time. In the end, she was humbled by her teacher's patience and integrity. The teacher understood that she wasn't there to simply give her student the answers she'd sought. She was there to gently steward her through her pilgrimage.

Everyone's healing path is their own; a good teacher will walk alongside you, hand in hand, but they know it's your task to take the medicine they are offering. Likewise, good teachers will not encourage a sense of dependency.

There may come a time when you understand that it's time to move on from working with a particular teacher. Perhaps your development surpasses their knowledge, or you may simply want to be with and integrate what you've learned. Or maybe your teacher feels you'd be better served elsewhere. A good teacher will be aware of this, and even before you bring it up, they might choose to let you know about other resources and teachers that might be able to support you at this stage.

Any teacher who clings to their students and doesn't incentivize them to be curious about what exists beyond their studies should raise some red flags. Just as a therapist might notice diminishing returns for their client after years of working together, a good teacher will recognize when it's time to respectfully transition a relationship, knowing that they can still be available in the future, as needed. They won't just release you into the darkness; they'll do what they can to make sure your journey ahead is filled with options and support that they might not be able to offer.

THEY VARY THEIR METHODS TO SUPPORT THEIR STUDENTS

This doesn't mean they weaken their wisdom in order to cater to their students' demands or level of receptivity. It simply means they are willing to disrupt conventional methods and models, such as whatever exists in the books, to make the teachings pertinent to a student's life and experiences. Sometimes, a teacher displays characteristics that might be considered unconventional. This is not to justify mistreatment or abuse. It is simply to remember some of what we might consider an unconventional approach is merely misunderstood.

For example, in the Andes, many wise teachers have the grace to perceive reality from a different and broader vision. After all, in Pacha philosophy, such people are adept at navigating different dimensions or worlds. Genuine Andean maestros have the capacity to see beyond what our human eyes can see. Thus, it's important to heed them—not necessarily with our rational minds but with our full sentipensante.

However, generally speaking, when a teacher chooses to dispense their teachings, it is important to rely on your own common sense and sentipensante. When you choose a teacher, you have the opportunity to strengthen and mature your adherence to unapologetic truth. If you are faced with a teacher whose methods seem strange or unconventional, you should always ask: "By doing this, will I be safe? Will my sentipensante be safe? Will my body be safe? Would I ask my children or grandchildren to do this? Would it be safe for them?"

It's good to remember that life is wild and unpredictable on its own without our having to move toward teachings that pull the rug out from underneath us or test our mettle. Sometimes, teachers create artificial scenarios for the sake of expediting a student's learning process, but this doesn't often help the student or their respective community.

Let's come back to Nature as a metaphor that demonstrates why discernment is so crucial. Over time, humans have evolved our agricultural methods and ways of growing food. But we are now discovering that such manipulation might actually be more harmful than helpful—from our bodies' inability to process manipulated foods. On the other hand, we have foods that have matured organically, in their own time. Such foods have demonstrated resilience to their environment. We can truly call these types of food holy sources. So, if we manipulate an environment so that the people and other beings within that environment experience a rapid and premature disruption, the adverse effects might outweigh the benefits. If we take such an approach and map it onto the spiritual path, we can see that it's also true that some ways of sending people into altered states can prove to be harmful—sometimes even resulting in psychotic breaks or delusions of grandeur.

I strongly believe that it's not an either/or situation. Disrupting conventional patterns of thinking in a non-harming way can be very effective. It can guide sincere students to recognize hidden blind spots and bring self-sabotaging cycles to an end. When such methods on the part of a teacher leave you curious and cause you to question things in a healthy way that supports your autonomy, they are working. However, if they make you question your very wellness, this is a sign that it might be time to part ways.

MIRROR THE JAGUAR

Finding a Teacher

- If you've been looking for a spiritual teacher or mentor (the latter entails a closer, more reciprocal relationship), what are your reasons? What has the search yielded so far?

- In the past, how have you sought out a mentor or teacher (e.g., knocking on doors, sending emails, paying for seminars)? What have been the results? Notice whether you've repeatedly encountered disappointment, which may indicate that you're searching in the wrong places or that other avenues might be more beneficial.

- What are the qualities that are most important to you in a teacher? List them. Afterwards, notice if there are qualities missing from your list that you could benefit from.

- What are the qualities that give you pause when it comes to working with a teacher? List them and reflect on whether you've encountered these qualities in the past.

- What are your nonnegotiables when it comes to working with a spiritual mentor or teacher? Notice whether you have any "rules" that are too rigid—such as the need for your teacher to be renowned in their field. In such a case, you might be limiting your options by not giving potent but obscure teachers the time of day. Sometimes, this is an indication that your vanity could be getting in the way.

WHAT IS AN ELDER?

I grew up in a culture that honored elders as the custodians of both sacred and practical knowledge. They had accumulated knowledge based on life experience. Of course, age isn't the only thing that marks an elder. Many people grow old without cultivating wisdom. At the same time, there are many young people who have lived through a great deal and have developed a mature perspective despite what might be construed as a lack of experience. Wisdom keepers can be elderly humans, and they can also be wise young people who have the grace to see and experience life from a different angle. Just as teachers come in a variety of forms, so do elders.

Is an elder the same as a teacher? Sometimes. However, many elders are not necessarily meant to teach, but to continue stoking the fires of ancestral wisdom and sharing the stories that connect us across time to our ancestors. In general, they might teach by example and inspiration more than through direct transmission. However, it is our responsibility to find ways to maintain the knowledge of our ancestral traditions, by honoring and observing their methods of doing and responding.

Nature is the ultimate elder. As previously discussed, everything has a nuna and everything is alive according to Pacha philosophy. When we come upon ancient mountains, trees, bodies of water, etc., we can choose to pay homage to the wisdom they hold and all that they have witnessed and encountered throughout their long lives.

Over the years, I have had the pleasure of sitting with many Andean elders as well as elders from other traditions. I have gained a great deal from their grace and steadfastness, but few of them would say that they are teachers. I once met an elder who said to me, "Every old person has a library of life experiences to share with their young, but let's not confuse that with the calling of a very few to store and safeguard and pass down the codes of knowledge for a particular tradition."

THE FEMININE AS ELDER AND TEACHER

There is a saying that is carved into my sentipensate: *Las lágrimas de una madre son saladas*. This means that when the tears of a mother are caused by the suffering of her children for their wrongdoing to her, it is a bad omen. The lesson is one of respect for your elders—especially for those in the role of your mother and grandmothers. There is an affiliation between respecting the women in our family and respecting Nature; both belong to the same life-giving force, after all. But unfortunately, our global treatment of the feminine aspects of Nature demonstrate that we are not in a balanced relationship with the feminine. This translates to our own distorted relationships with our mothers and grandmothers, as well as the ways in which we extract from the Earth without a sense of care, gratitude, and respect.

There's another saying: *Las oraciones de una madre y abuelita son milagrosas* or, "The prayers of a mother and grandmother are miraculous." I can personally say that I am alive and well due to my mother's and grandmothers' faith and prayers. Of course, we are all human and carry our own flaws and wounds; with the principle of correspondence, we carry both the victim and the perpetrator within us. But thanks to the maternal role they play in our lives, mothers, grandmothers, and caretakers have a special bond with their children. They have access to the secrets of easing our pain and rejoicing in our victories.

Although I grew up in a heavily Catholic environment in which misunderstandings and misinformation abounded with respect to our sacred Andean traditions, the syncretic essence of our religious worship meant that I had access to both parts of my heritage. Incense, palo santo, and agua florida took up their space in altars with Bibles, rosaries, and statues of the Virgin Mary. My dear abuelitas carried the wisdom of their lineage with them, and in so doing, they found ways to teach me invaluable lessons.

One of my abuelitas valued the power of Nature in healing. She was a pious woman to whom many community members turned for advice, especially when it came to healing their young. My grandmother performed special care for babies and small children, and she also opened her home to whomever needed shelter or food. She had a strong belief in *la olla milagrosa*, or "the miraculous cooking pot;" she'd cook for four people, but her meal would be capable of nourishing twenty. This abuelita also taught me the secrets of herbs and food, the wisdom of weaving, and the importance of moving backwards in order to move forward.

My other abuelita was a master of adaptability and confidence. She was smart, determined, and wise beyond her years. Although she was diminutive in stature, she was definitely not the kind of woman to be crossed or trifled with. She was a resourceful Nature lover who taught me how to care for the trees and respect the thorns of beautiful and therapeutic flowers and plants. She loved to share her stories, and she always treated me as her equal and welcomed all my questions. To the best of her ability, she taught me to honor my voice and cultivate a mind on my own.

Although both of my grandmothers, my original maestras, are on the other side in *Uku Pacha* (the underworld or realm of the dead), I continue to feel them with me. I know they have not left. I may not see them, but I feel them and receive their messages. In fact, I've come to regard the presence of the colibrí, or hummingbird, as a sign that my grandmothers are sending me messages. Often, I'll receive an instantaneous download of knowledge in the form of insights and guidance when I see a hummingbird; this allows me to feel the wisdom of my abuelitas' spiritual messages, as well as their love. When you honor your dead, they become palpable spiritual forces that continue to offer their support in the unseen realm.

To this day, when I am in the midst of any sort of unbearable predicament, I continue to call on the matriarchs in my life, who were complete—albeit imperfect—embodiments of love, grace, humility, and devotion. When I need to put anything into perspective, I might ask: What would my elders do in this situation? What would my abuelitas do or not do?

It is important to honor all our elders, but how do you honor the role of the feminine as elder in your own life? As I've mentioned throughout this book, we are in a time during which long-standing cycles are adjusting. Patterns are breaking, which is necessary in order for new possibilities to be birthed. For thousands of years, we've been in the stranglehold of almost exclusively patriarchal structures, almost as if we were raised by a single father. We have been in a state of widespread imbalance. This has been an era in which the father has been given broader honor, typically in the form of organized religion and other structures that magnify the traditionally masculine over the feminine. We have been motherless and desperately searching for maternal care and love. It isn't that one way is better than the other; on the contrary, we are looking for complementary structures and systems, which are necessary to reach harmony and balance in Nature and the spiritual realm.

As we women continue to embrace our own ways of teaching and reclaiming our truth, I believe that we will all eventually come into a more harmonious relationship with the feminine. The matriarchs of our communities, societies, cultures, and wisdom traditions will have the stronger presence they are meant to embody. By this, I don't mean to say that there will be a "goddess" who supplants the masculine, for we need balance in order to experience true harmony. However, the energy of the feminine aspect of Nature is regaining the ground that is so desperately needed in our days. Even as we move into what can feel like a chaotic period of transitioning out of the current cycle, we can take heart and remember the promise of balance and sacred reciprocity.

EMBODY THE JAGUAR
Honoring Your Teachers and Elders

- Honor your teachers: You can do this by maintaining constant communication and asking, "What do you need? How can I be of service?" This is an act of sacred reciprocity that honors the energetic exchange between you. Knowing that wealth does not rest merely in material possessions, you can serve these teachers who have committed their own lives to service. For example, if you're tech-savvy, you might offer your teacher help with designing a website or completing tasks on the computer.

Sacred Reciprocity

Name of Teacher / Elder	What Does the Teacher / Elder Need?	How I Can Serve with My Skills and Resources
Teacher / Elder 1	Monthly food Light cleaning Cleaning supplies	I have extra money and time this month
Teacher / Elder 2	Translation Transportation to appointments	I'm bilingual and have a car and time
Teacher / Elder 3	Tech support for website and social media	I'm tech-savvy and have an extra laptop

- Honor your elders: For elders who are deceased (such as grandmothers, grandfathers, or other beloved people), you might choose to pray to or communicate with them on a daily basis. For example, I light candles and bring flowers to my altar for deceased elders, in order to honor them and the ways they continue to inspire me. If I am outside and feel the wind, I call them in and whisper blessings and prayers of gratitude and love. For those who are still alive, I might honor their needs by being attentive to their preferences. For example, I don't bring someone flowers if that's not what they like. Create sacred contracts that help you maintain your sense of service to the beloved elders in your life by honoring your personal connection and offering them what brings them joy.

9

EMBRACING YOUR MEDICINE AND FINDING SPIRITUAL BALANCE

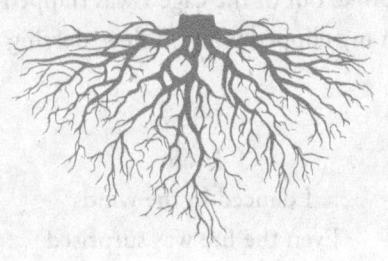

Legacy

Can you see me?
Can you feel me?
Can you hear me?

I escaped from her in tears
because I was afraid that she would tear me apart

I escaped to the mountains, trying to hide
I jumped into the lake, knowing I can't swim
I broke out of the cage I was trapped in
and with my clipped wings, I flew, defying the odds

I flew
I rose
I danced in the winds
Even the fire was surprised

The grandmother Jaguar, standing at the edge of life
with manta and claws all worn out from so much fighting
is looking at me with pride

I'm looking at you with pride
Can you please do the same?

Oh, little one, beauty of my heart
piece of heaven on earth
It's time to see you sprout
It's your time!

You will feel alone
You will encounter setbacks

But remember, alone you are not
because my manta and my claws, all worn out,
I'm leaving with you

Our healing is by no means a purely personal endeavor. It must always be connected to the world around us, and to how we are engaging in sacred reciprocity with humanity and all of Nature. Ultimately, it is our responsibility to bridge our healing with service to our greater *ayllu* (family and community in Quechua).

In this final chapter, beloved friend, we'll investigate what it means to walk with a straight back as we weave our own manta and move our gifts forward in the world. This must occur in tandem with honing our capacity to walk backwards, with care and awareness of the past and where we come from.

First, we have to investigate what it means to locate, find, reconcile, and utilize our specific medicine in service to the world. This isn't something you can discover through a weekend workshop or by studying the trending social media campaigns. Nor is it necessarily tied to your livelihood. It is the awareness that comes from the blood, sweat, and tears of your reconciliation pilgrimage.

You learn about your gifts when you are fully able to accept that *you* are also the medicine. When you come in contact with the jaguar—even though it may feel like a terrifying journey that rips you in a million different pieces and causes you to question everything you once thought to be true—you are wrapped in the manta of your innate nature and grace. Bathed in the tears and forged in the fire of your ancestors, human and non-human, you emerge as an autonomous being who knows your value and worth. Your primal realizations nourish you with the understanding that you have something meaningful to give . . . and it may not look exactly the way you had once envisioned! I certainly have found this to be true for my own journey.

If we have a crisis in confidence, we must resource ourselves and recognize that our sovereignty is our birthright, and our sense of purpose is a part of this. We also have to recognize that some of us may not know that we are going through a crisis in confidence, especially if we are accustomed to feeling like we have nothing to offer. This is why it's so invigorating to develop an understanding of purpose through the framework of our elemental and ancestral connections, and the fact that we are innately woven into Nature.

Here, I'd like to reframe the word *purpose*, beloved friend. In this chapter, we will operate under the premise that every single one of us has purpose, simply because we are here. Our purpose is woven into our very existence. Everything in Pacha has purpose. With a sense of ritual, we can return to Nature anything that creates imbalance and disrupts harmony. We can also ask Nature to reestablish order in our lives if we feel lost or adrift.

I also want to define the idea of the *roles* we carry in this plane of existence. Every role we might have—mother, daughter, spouse, teacher, etc.—is meant to serve us and those who are a part of our ayllu. No role is rigid; it is mobile and a constant part of a cycle.

Then, there is our *vocation*. Whereas purpose is associated with our sense of connection to meaning, vocation is all about fulfilling that meaning through action. Our vocation may be what we do for our livelihood or not, but it's always connected to using our gifts in an enjoyable and actionable way. Throughout this chapter, I use the term *true vocation* to describe what may be commonly referred to as *purpose*. Of course, our true vocation is something that can evolve over the years, too. We may not have a single vocation, which is why it's good to wake up from the dream and sprout anew from wholesome seeds, free of false definitions.

Finally, there is *service*. When we are deeply connected to our vocation, we are being of service.

When we embody the jaguar, we start to look at the world differently. It becomes more possible to feel our purpose, to embrace our roles, to know our true vocation, and to share our gifts from a truly generous place, in a large and unapologetic way—not in terms of the number of people we're sharing with but in terms of the expression of sweet love, joy, and service that accompanies our offering. When we do this, we experience the grace of our medicine—which I define as the elixir that is the result of our purpose, roles, true vocation, and service being in alignment. It is crucial to recognize that accessing our medicine is our solemn commitment to assisting others—not by attempting to seek recognition but by truly supporting others to recover or reestablish their own balance.

In addition, we must continue to ask ourselves what it looks like to live in a state of spiritual balance and harmony. We don't need to reject the material world to achieve balance, but we do need to come into a reconciliation between the material and spiritual realms. Our ideas about "abundance" have often been skewed by our wounding, as well as the idea that we must have more, more, more, in order to experience our intrinsic worth. Beloved friend, this isn't true! Understandably, many of us are doing so in order to leave financial hardships behind, but the pressure to succeed in the material world can disconnect us from Nature.

All of this work entails weaving ourselves back into Nature over and over again, as it can guide us to heal our wounds. When we do this, we are enjoined to seek what we need and to create a world where all beings have what they need. By doing so, we fulfill the principles of relationality and complementarity that are a part of Sumaq Kawsay; that is, what impacts one of us impacts the rest.

KNOWING YOUR TRUE VOCATION AND SHARING YOUR GIFTS

Many of my clients are people who have a strong sense of a calling . . . but they can't always identify what that calling is. They are passionate and driven by their desire to be of service, but many of them also feel lost and disconnected from a sense of deeper meaning.

I know it is easy to fall under the mistaken belief that we have lost a sense of direction. However, when we accept that we humans are Pacha in and of itself—literally, Nature discovering, creating, and organizing itself—it is hard to remain captive to that spell! We are literally human beings *doing*. Even when things feel still, Nature is unceasingly in motion, evolving and transforming. We are in a state of constant change, even though our essence remains stable. We are meant to sojourn through time and space with an enthusiastic commitment to learning, growing, and creating—which is not the same as the mentality of achievement and accomplishment that is so often tied to the notion of "purpose."

If our sentipensante is feeling fragmented, it will become difficult to honor and reconcile with our true medicine. This is when it's time to call our nuna back. When life feels like it is moving in all directions, we have to remember that we are Nature, and we're being called to bring ourselves back into balance and harmony.

Sometimes, it's a matter of changing our orientation and direction. One of my clients, Gloria, learned that she carries more than one medicine, which was a new realization to her. She was a physician, but as she was getting older, she felt more drawn to teaching young doctors about self-care and ethics. At first, she was resistant to the idea of leaving her successful career to teach, but through our work together, she came to accept that she was moving into a different phase of life that was asking her to honor her burgeoning medicine as a teacher. Gloria's migrant parents had drilled it into her that her only way to access a sense of meaning was to be successful. Thankfully, by working through her early wounding from growing up with financial hardships and scarcity and calling her nuna back, she developed the confidence to move toward her current calling, which was not as lucrative but brought her a sense of satisfaction beyond her wildest dreams.

Gloria was fortunate to be able to weave a new, truer vocation from her gifts, but I want to emphasize that our true vocation isn't always the same as the thing we do for a living! For example, Gloria's close friend,

Brian, is also a physician who happens to be an extremely talented singer and pianist. Brian is enthusiastic about being a physician—and he's not about to quit his day job anytime soon to pursue being a songwriter. At the same time, the healing aspect of Brian's music flows into his work as a physician.

But what if you don't feel you have a gift, passion, or true vocation you can easily identify? I recall having a client, Nora, who told me she'd read all the self-help books, hoping she could finally find what she was "good" at. She was afraid that if she didn't discover it soon, it would be too late. But then, one day, as she stood in the middle of her dining room with family and friends all around her, she realized she'd been living inside her true vocation for years without realizing it. Nora excitedly told me, "I knew I was in my element—living as my most authentic, grateful, harmonious self—when I was bringing my favorite people together and making sure they were nourished, well-fed, comfortable, and warmed by sweet, unconditional love. I just hadn't realized that this was actually important!"

What we love *is* important. What feeds us and comes naturally to us *is* important. That which lights us up and feels so effortless that we don't think twice about doing it *is* important. Because *we* are important, and we deserve to feel fulfilled and like we're living inside the most expansive expression of who we are . . . which is our ultimate true vocation.

We are as valuable as the trees, as ferocious as the fire that burns, as whole and beautiful as the waters, as vital as the air we need to breathe. We come from Nature, and when we remember this, we reconnect with who we truly are.

I often say to the young people in my inner circle: "You need to know where you come from so you know where you're going." Yes, that includes our past and our lineage, but it's also about recollecting that we *are* Pacha. We are the daughters and sons of the sun, the water, the fire, the winds, and the earth—and if we are embodying all of this, then we are living inside and from our true vocation.

WHAT DOES IT MEAN TO BE OF SERVICE?

Something I have thought about a lot lately is the idea of *help*. Many of us who wish to be of service desire to "help" others. However, this paradigm limits us, because it places helpers on a pedestal and imagines that those being helped are lacking agency. Help can also come with a sense of entitlement from the person receiving it, and the pretense of authority from the one giving it. It creates uneven ground, where there may be certain expectations on either side. A word supported by Pacha philosophy that I prefer and I'm relearning to use is *support*.

In Pacha philosophy, we honor relationality. We are all supporting one another in an intricate ecosystem of relationships. If I am truly embodying the manta of Pacha and I am Pacha itself, I am invited to seek out harmony and reciprocity. I offer my service to anyone who needs it, and in the capacity that I can manage—not to impose my practices or beliefs on anyone, but to support them in walking their own autonomous path.

To be of service, it's also good to walk the middle path between our individual gifts and the good of the collective. In fact, Andean wisdom, passed down through the ages, demonstrates that neither pure individualism nor pure collectivism is the right answer. Too much of an emphasis in either direction can be risky. In the case of offering service and support, we might overly fixate on thinking how wonderful we are for being champions of the poor and downtrodden—or we might eliminate our own needs and become boundaryless in our desire to serve others. This is when our vocation becomes self-glorification or servitude!

Pacha philosophy recognizes that individuals and communities are meant to work in conjunction. The individual cares for others, and the community as a whole supports every individual. After all, the sources of well-being are people and Nature brought together in the spirit of service. We allow ourselves to enter relationships of reciprocity, so that we are receiving exactly what we need and giving what uplifts us and the people around us. We engage in collaborative decision-making, rather than taking it upon ourselves to do everything alone. We know that service is a part of who we are and a source of our intrinsic wellness. We experience wellness when our community experiences wellness.

Here, I want to emphasize that service doesn't necessarily look like devoting our lives to a particular cause or group of people. We are all interconnected, and even if we may not feel that we are doing something for others, we are. All we need to do is turn to the great nurturer of all beings, Nature. Little creatures and wildlife are facing the devastation of their habitats, yet the bees are still continuing to pollinate the flowers and the crops we humans need to survive. The ants are still doing their job of turning and aerating soil so that the water and oxygen can reach the roots of the plants that sustain us.

If we look closely, we can see that all of us have a similar role. Some are nurses who take care of the brood. Others are janitors who clean the hive. Still others are foragers who gather nectar to make honey. In this way, we are all woven into Nature's manta in relationships of service and reciprocity, regardless of whether we are aware of them . . . although it is certainly good to exercise greater awareness!

Still, I have had clients ask, "What if I want to be of service but I find that I am excluding certain people? Does that mean I haven't done enough work on myself?" My answer is, "Not necessarily."

I once worked with a client, Naomi, who was helping people in the prison system with transformative inner healing. However, she had been a victim of violent assault at a younger age, so she found it very difficult to work with men who had been incarcerated for assaulting women. Naomi felt guilty that she was excluding these men from her work. I understood her concerns, but I also gently said, "You may not get to a place where you feel comfortable working with these men. And yes, while it's true that our service is transformative when we don't limit it to a certain group we see as 'deserving,' you can be sweet to yourself and honor your limitations right now. Recognize that even if you aren't comfortable working with such men, you wish them wellness and no harm." This was freeing for Naomi, who continued to come back to the KARE method to examine some of the tender wounds from her past.

Sometimes, we have the mistaken notion that we are too broken and fragmented to be of service to others, but this isn't true. It's good to continue to "KARE" for ourselves through our perceived limitations. It's also good to go through the cycle of facing the places where we have been harmed and wounded. However, this is not meant to be permanent. Perhaps one of the greatest acts of service we can perform is doing the internal healing to reclaim our wholeness—for it assists us to reconnect with the greater manta, and to the possibility of collective healing.

MIRROR THE JAGUAR

Accessing Your Medicine

- What would you say your gifts are? How do they contribute to your true vocation and sense of service? How do they give you a sense of purpose and meaning? Try not to think too much about the answers. Use your sentipensante to spontaneously journal your responses.

- In what ways can you bring the elements of Nature into an understanding of what it means to live in your true vocation, sharing your gifts with others? This doesn't have to be extravagant. For example, as you shower, you can intentionally call upon water to cleanse and guide you, so that you might integrate your true vocation into your sentipensante.

- Try conversing with the elements to better know your gifts, true vocation, and service to the world. For example, what is the water in your body telling you? Just as you explored in the exercises in chapter 2, is there a particular element you feel most drawn to at this time? How would it advise you?

- The major principles of Sumaq Kawsay—relationality, complementarity, correspondence, reciprocity, and cyclicality—offer a model of coexistence without which

Nature's balance would be disrupted. For example, we are all woven from the elements. Fire might seem disconnected from air, but it needs oxygen from the air in order to burn; it might also seem disconnected from water, but it has the capacity to create water vapor when it burns. Together, the elements create a balanced, interconnected Pacha, where nothing stands alone. How can you work with these natural principles to be of service to the world?

- If you are having difficulty connecting to your true vocation and deeper gifts, ask these basic questions:
    - What do I want?
    - What do I need?
    - What makes me happy?
    - If I knew it was my last day on Earth, what would I regret not having done?

ENERGETIC EXCHANGE

I knew long ago that my first published book (the one you hold in your hands, beloved friend) would be my act of service and commitment in honor of the matriarchs on the horizon—the ones who are awakening to graciously offer their medicine wherever it may be needed, and to weave the manta of sacred tradition and Nature's wisdom that the world is so deeply yearning for.

Many of us struggle with the mental fixation of deficiency that makes the idea of abundance, reciprocal exchange, and embodying our true vocation in service to others difficult for us.

If our mental fixation has been one of scarcity, how do we come into a new relationship with abundance? We do so by recognizing that there must be an energetic exchange between us and the ones receiving our medicine. This may not come in the form of money, but it must be something that offers us what we need, so that we have the energy and sustenance to keep giving.

One of my clients, Regina, was a doula who was dedicated to supporting her clients to learn more about their bodies and what they needed throughout the process of gestating a child in their wombs. However, because she was also in a full-time master's program to supplement her knowledge, she quickly ended up feeling depleted of time and energy. And although Regina had intentionally set her offerings at the lower end and created a tiered pricing structure in order to make them accessible to the people in her community who needed them, she began to feel resentful toward her clients, who seemed to demand her attention and care at all times of the day. In addition, her relationship was beginning to suffer because she was so burned out; her partner suggested that she take a break or change something about her business strategy. "When are you going to take care of *you*?" he asked. Her sentipensante was moving her to make a decision that she didn't feel comfortable with. Finally, her nuna made the choice for her.

Regina began to suffer from nervous anxiety, and her body broke out in hives. That was when she sought me out. Some of her childhood wounds arose during our work together. She shared that, because she was the oldest of five, she'd learned from a young age to care for others, and this was the beginning of neglecting herself. Regina had never learned to create sacred boundaries, which give us clarity about how we want to be treated and which people and activities we accept into our orbit. When sacred boundaries don't exist or are eroded, we are at the behest of other people and their demands. But when we institute sacred boundaries, we cultivate a sustainable way to heal ourselves—because we are taking back our autonomy. She realized that she'd been depleting herself, emotionally and financially, to the extent that she had even begun to question whether any of it was worth it. Through our work together, Regina realized that she needed to find a new way to offer her service and medicine.

Like a lot of the women I work with, Regina was an empath who was programmed to take on too great of a burden without asking for very much in return, including time for herself. The truth was, her work with pregnant women and reproductive health *had* been her lifelong gift and true vocation—but she hadn't realized that to make it her service, she also needed to ensure that her own needs were taken care of!

In Pacha philosophy, there is a concept known as *ayni*, which roughly translates to "sacred reciprocity and mutuality." Of course, ayni is a practice that was originally done to benefit all members of the ayllu, so applying it to modern-day business can be complex—but with integrity and intention, it's possible.

I explained to Regina that I had gone through a similar process of realizing that the practice of ayni means that all parties within an exchange are benefited—even the one giving. I told her, "As much as I want to cultivate my gifts, my service doesn't belong to me. I'm just a vessel, and I have to be prudent about making sure the 'vessel' is as healthy and whole as it can be." With that metaphor, she finally got it.

We talked through her desire to be fairly compensated for her work and ways that people who wanted her services could seek her out. The dilemma was that some of Regina's clients who were paying close to nothing were leveraging her generosity. I reminded her that the energetic exchange didn't necessarily need to be in the form of money, but there had to be a relationship of balance and mutuality that she was able to clearly communicate or she'd continue to feel drained. Regina determined that she needed guidance to restructure her business, so she decided that while she'd keep her low and tiered pricing, she'd seek out support in gathering supplies, building her website, and increasing her social media presence. Thankfully, the clients who were benefiting from her generous rates signed up to offer this support, which ended up gaining her new clients who were able to compensate her for her services at the standard rate.

In addition, Regina learned the value of taking sacred time to care for herself. "I'm very introverted and find solace in solitude and silence," she said, "but my family constantly made me feel there was something wrong with my desire to be alone from time to time. I was conditioned to constantly serve other people, which meant I never had a moment to myself. To this day, I worry that wanting 'me' time is selfish."

As Regina learned, building sacred boundaries that enable us to develop a trusting and compassionate connection with our bodies and our sentipensante is not easy, especially if we come from families with dynamics that lack a neutral space for us to process our experiences—as well as our wants and needs.

However, as a doula and someone supporting the process of bringing life into the world, Regina had to respect that fruitful solitude is often necessary in order to absorb Nature's messages and fill our own cup. In fact, solitude can make many introverts feel more connected, whereas constant interaction with others can reinforce the sense of greater fragmentation and loneliness. Connecting with the elements, the environment around us, and the multiverse of Pacha is deeply nourishing and brings us back into balance with ourselves. Regina learned to value her sacred "me" time and to set sacred boundaries around it that her friends, family, and clients respected. As I explained to Regina, "Most people have no idea what affects you, because it is your responsibility to provide clarity as to how you wish to be treated." I also guided Regina to look at the places where she tended to over-give, as these were also places where she was likely bypassing her own issues and need for healing.

Please remember that in your own experiences, whether you are the one giving or the one receiving, it's crucial to be thoughtful about whether your activities are depleting you if you're the one giving, or if they are causing depletion in those who may be offering support. When we don't maintain sacred boundaries, the result can be devastating, as it prevents us from properly sharing our gifts, virtues, and medicine with the world. This is why it's crucial to partake in transactions that allow us to feel sincerely fulfilled and recharged.

Again, this goes beyond the exchange of money; it also gets into questions of when we may be transgressing against our own or another's autonomy. In the manta of life, we are all precious and necessary, so be intentional about the circumstances under which you are offering your medicine or being nurtured by another's. Is there a respectful mutuality? Are you able to recognize and honor your own needs with your full sentipensante? It is not selfish to have needs. All of Nature's children have needs, and being aware of your own will allow you to be a clear and responsible vessel in which your gifts may flourish.

CELEBRATING OUR ABUNDANCE

With the individualism commonly associated with Western cultures, there can be a sense of constantly needing to get somewhere. We are programmed to be wrapped up in the idea of success and having "more." However, this model of success usually entails a continued planning for some far-off future that we never seem to actually reach. We aren't encouraged to embrace the factual reality unfolding, which is tantamount to embodying the jaguar in the realm of living and existence and not being so attached to outcomes.

Something I have personally discovered is that the experience of abundance is connected to celebration and the recognition of cycles in our lives. Pacha philosophy tells us that everything occurs in cycles in Nature and—rather than clinging to the idea of having more, more, more and getting to a pinnacle of success that we feel we haven't yet reached—we must learn to celebrate how far we've come.

For decades, I didn't know what this meant. So today, I am learning to celebrate my learning and to see that I'm exactly where I need to be! Now, I understand what it means to complete a cycle before moving on to the "next thing." We must properly honor all aspects of the cycle that we find ourselves in, which may include experiences of frustration, hardship, and feeling like we haven't arrived at our desired destination. Although it can be difficult to feel this when we're in the midst of challenges, by remembering that life operates on the principles of complementarity and correspondence, we can compassionately accept that light and darkness coexist. When we properly celebrate where we are in the cycle, including the end of any particular cycle in our lives, we face life with unapologetic truth. We are able to celebrate both our so-called failures and successes, and to know that we did our very best for ourselves and our community with whatever we had.

Celebration also enables us to reorient to our sense of service to others. So often in today's modern world, sharing our achievements is centered around ourselves. Celebrating the end of cycles is a wildly different approach. It guides us to see the abundance that already exists in our lives.

Beloved friend, you are probably aware of the manifestation practices that exist in the realm of spirituality and the "new age" movement. Many of them are meaningful and can free us from the chains of scarcity in our lives. But in what ways, from your experience, might these approaches be limited? It's good to consider this for ourselves, with as much radical intimacy and unapologetic honesty as we can.

As Pacha philosophy tells us, we are constantly in a state of co-creation, because this is our fundamental nature. It's what defines our role as human beings. After all, Pacha is not just an environment that is external to us—it is a part of us and we are part of it. When we recognize this, we don't try to "get more" to appease our feelings of insecurity and scarcity. We realize that abundance doesn't end with us, nor with our worries and concerns about material prosperity. It is about taking decisive action to care for our natural environments, as well as our fellow human beings, with the integrity and respect they deserve.

Often, people assume that the act of co-creation has a prerequisite of material success. It's true that dire circumstances like poverty, systemic injustices, and individual hardship are forces that we need to continually acknowledge and reckon with. At the same time, even in the most devastating situations, we still have the capacity to co-create our environment. Every little action we take in our current state matters. For example, take somebody who has a long prison sentence. Their goal might be to do whatever they can to get out of these circumstances, but realistically, in order to reconcile with the state of inner peace that impacts how they deal with their outer circumstances, they need to engage in a mature intervention that helps them to show up in that environment exactly as they are. This may include mourning their old life, as well as the actions that brought them to this place. Even in seemingly constrained spaces, we have the capacity to co-create with life.

This experience of celebrating exactly where we are in the cycle helps us to make tangible differences in our lives. We're not just focusing on getting to the very next thing. Rather, we recognize our agency every step of the way. We realize that we are Pacha itself. We are rightful heirs of all the cycles of Nature, including the plenitude of abundance in our harvesting seasons.

My own experience of abundance is connected to my capacity to support others, including the people in my community and the matriarchs on the horizon. Our mental fixation on scarcity leads us all to feel "poor" in one way or another, even if we do have some financial stability. The remedy is to recognize that we ourselves are just as valuable as the trees, just as impressive as the mountains. When we embrace that awareness of our own value and abundance, we can break free of our conditioning around scarcity and competition. This recognition can lead you to rethink the whole idea of status, as well as your beliefs about abundance. All of us have sweet seeds of greatness within us, so on some level, all of us are abundant.

An essential way to celebrate our abundance is to recognize the importance of the land and those who directly labor with and on land. In many societies across the world, land laborers are frequently viewed as unskilled, and due to limited opportunities, tend to be at the bottom of the economic hierarchy. But when we practice within Pacha philosophy and other traditions that respect the Earth, we recognize that those who are in communion with the land are demonstrating a potent sacred contract that all of us can choose to learn from. Within Andean codes, abundance is related to how much grace an ayllu will receive in the *cosecha* (harvest). This is why we make our own sacred contracts—so that Pachamama can open her mouth/heart to receive and in reciprocity give us what we need.

Again, this reflection on abundance requires that we recognize there will be times of incubation and times of birthing. But everything, including our pain and sorrow, will follow its cycle to a close. When we choose to celebrate every position we assume on the circle of life, we start to see that true abundance isn't about money, conventional success, receiving recognition, or being entitled to luxury objects. We may be limited with our material resources, but we can still celebrate the abundance into which we are naturally woven.

FINDING SPIRITUAL BALANCE

How do we find a sense of spiritual balance overall, within ourselves and with the world around us, especially in times of transitions and crisis? Here are three specific and impactful ways that you can experience greater harmony and a persistent sense of being woven into the manta of life.

HONOR THE MEDICINES YOU CHOOSE TO TAKE

In order to give freely of our medicine, we must also be aware of the medicines that are nourishing us. This is an act of sacred reciprocity that honors both what we have to give, as well as what we have received. Giving and receiving are interconnected in a feedback loop, which is why being aware of our consumption and of the medicine we are taking into ourselves is so important—it impacts our own sense of service in the world.

Individual healing can only take us so far. Until it is connected to the collective goal of well living for all of Nature's children, it will only appear to be for the fortunate few, while the rest of us remain in survival mode. This is why it is crucial to be attentive to the medicines we are taking—which may encompass plant medicine, healing therapies, and modalities for taming the mind and enhancing our spiritual connection—as well as their history and context. We must not be casual about the medicines we are embracing, ingesting, injecting, and inhaling. As we engage with them, we also engage with their nuna—as well as the nuna of all those who may have died to protect the medicine, and all those who may have killed to annihilate it.

Please remember that a superficial engagement with the medicines that you look to for healing can lead to a superficial understanding of your true vocation. By situating yourself in the larger manta of life, you demonstrate a greater awareness of and respect for Pacha and a great awareness of and respect for yourself.

BE GENEROUS AND GRATEFUL

I once worked with a financially stable client named Sofia, who came to me because she was experiencing a deep sense of deficiency and scarcity in her life with respect to relationships, work, and overall life satisfaction. "I feel like I don't have anything I really want," she explained. Interestingly, Sofia had ample resources and income, but she had grown up with a great deal of financial insecurity. She had a tendency to hoard money in order to feel secure. But this sense of "hoarding" had resulted in a mental fixation that was quite frugal. Although she had a great deal of resources, beyond just her finances, she didn't think any of it was enough. She was focused on how little she had, which meant that her behaviors lacked generosity—which caused the people in her life to hold her at a distance.

I suggested that Sofia attempt to do something nice for someone in her life, and to designate the amount of money she felt comfortable spending—an amount that would allow her to feel abundant without being concerned that she might become "broke." Sofia had expressed that she wished to cultivate a closer relationship with her mother, so she decided that she'd plan a trip for them both. Amazingly, she returned from that trip a transformed woman. Instead of shopping around for the cheapest hotel, Sofia challenged herself to give this gift from a place of true abundance—and therefore, true generosity. After that trip, Sofia revealed that her relationship with her mother and other people in her life improved astronomically. She actually felt like she belonged to a family. Her relationship with money also changed. Instead of holding on so tightly to her material resources, she felt freer to be generous and to use her financial freedom to create greater happiness and ease around her.

"What I realized was that giving was an expression of my gratitude," she shared with me. "I had never gotten a chance to tell my mother how grateful I was for all the sacrifices she made for me and my siblings. When I realized that 'sharing the wealth,' so to speak, was a way of thanking her—and when I saw that I hadn't done this because I was so scared of losing everything I had, I knew that I had the power to change an old pattern. I could choose sweet love over fear, knowing that I really did have enough."

As Sofia discovered, expressing gratitude guides us to share abundance. We recognize that our service to others is nothing less than service to ourselves; after all, our threads are intertwined in the same manta. The great thing about this approach is that it also makes us much more conscious of the medicine in our midst; we want to protect it and to treat everything around us as part of a sacred exchange.

Gratitude and generosity toward our ayllu is an expression of Sumaq Kawsay that is deeply rooted in Andean and Latin American communities. It doesn't end with saying "thank you." It lives on in our memory, offering timelessness to good deeds and ensuring that we honor those proximate to us, including deceased loved ones. Gratitude and generosity continue to bear fruit, which is why it's good to practice both of them in our lives, no matter what we're going through.

"Try not to be ungrateful," my mother constantly tells me. "Be thankful for the good and for the bad. Be thankful for the things that happened even when your seed wasn't here to witness it."

Expressing gratitude and generosity is a way of embodying balance in the same ways as Nature. We can do so by giving and receiving freely, without expecting anything in return. I especially cherish seeing my vegetables growing from the earth, generously offering their seeds and reminding me of the bounty that exists all around me—and that I seek to replicate in my own sentipensante and engagement with the worlds within and without.

HONOR CYCLES

As I've already mentioned, one of the main principles of Sumaq Kawsay is the recognition of the cyclical nature of life. There is a time to mourn, and a time to celebrate; a time to harvest, and a time to economize. Nature's essential balance reminds us that we cannot expect a cycle of continuous growth or continuous scarcity. What goes up must come down. Each season gives way to the next one. And as we honor the cyclical truths of Pacha, we weave ourselves into all our experiences, from being cared for to being the caregivers. We honor the contrasting hues and flavors of life. We come into a radical intimacy with all our emotions, dense and smooth, so that we can attune to the full experience of Pacha.

There is a celebratory aspect to honoring cycles. Yes, we honor the end of a cycle—just as we observe the end of each season, or the end of a year, or the end of a specific phase of life. But ideally, we are able to celebrate, no matter where we are in the cycle—whether we're in the midst of a sensual, life-affirming "summer" or in the darkest night of a grief-soaked "winter." Even our grief can be celebrated as nourishment for future seasons.

Take a moment to go outside and observe the cycles of Nature. Nature is always in a state of celebration, no matter what is happening. In the midst of a thunderous downpour, the earth is being nourished. In the midst of a ravenous fire, seeds that require extreme heat or chemical signals from smoke and charred plants in order to germinate are moving from dormancy to life.

We can't control what's going to happen next, but we can control our response to wherever we are in the cycle. We can trust that we have the tools and the sentipensante to respond to life . . . always with the recognition that, even though our physical body will eventually dissolve and return to the elements, we can move through our existence with the grace of our eternal essence always shining through.

EMBODY THE JAGUAR
Celebrating the Cycle of Life

When we are out of balance, we may sometimes feel that something is missing. When we experience this, it may mean that we have come to the end of a particular cycle in our life and it's time to celebrate. The cyclical nature of Pacha is one of the major principles of Sumaq Kawsay. We can learn to "close the loop" of the cycle we are in and accept it. You can make the following sacred contract to celebrate wherever you are in the cycle:

- First, determine where you are in your own personal cycle. Are you in a state of giving or receiving? Starting or ending? Planting or harvesting? You may relate to these questions in different ways depending on the aspect you are looking at (e.g., work, relationships, home), but try to apply this to the bigger picture of your life.

- Wherever you are, ask yourself: *What do I want? What do I need?* Keep in mind the dense and smooth emotions you may be feeling. You may wish to dialogue with your dense emotions to get a sense of how they may wish to be soothed.

- What does celebration look and feel like for you? List your favorite ways to celebrate.

- Use the elements of Nature to create a sacred contract of celebration, remembering we can always find ways to celebrate, exactly where we are. Perhaps you feel you are "in the dark," so to speak. This can necessitate a symbolic action, such as planting a seed, which grows in the dark as it moves toward the sun. Or perhaps you are ending a relationship, which may lead to a bonfire celebration in which you and loved ones "offer" that which you are ready to let go of while experiencing the supportive warmth that comes from letting go.

- Consider creating sacred contracts to observe cycles in Nature: equinoxes, solstices, moon cycles, and other moments that help you to situate yourself in the manta of life. Again, use the elements of Nature as foundational tools to help you mark the passage of time.

CONCLUSION

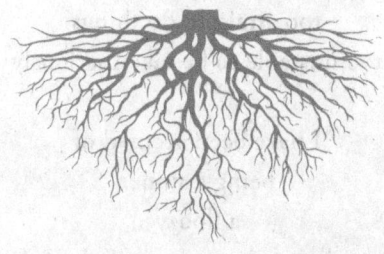

Awakening Matriarchs

Many forces assure me
that I am broken and damaged
dumb and stupid, deficient
unloveable, insignificant
not enough, a second-class human
without a mind of my own
and too emotional
too afraid to do things
too unstable to be taken seriously

I have been accused of
being a sinner
a floozy
who needs repentance to be holy and pure
a bitch
a hellcat
a radical loose cannon when I speak up

My mistakes have served as a curse that filters the treatment
I had to learn to endure

And you are asking me to be quiet now that I have woken up?
Why do you think I'd want to do that?

It took centuries to break the spell I was put in
whips on backs that I now incarnate
screams of the uterus obligated to be silent

The strength to resist losing my integrity
is what moves me
now that I walk revived

So please don't be surprised
that my actions look like a rebellion,
when in reality it is the overdue expression
of who I was meant to be

My voice, my actions, and my existence
are not an inconvenience

I'm not here to satisfy your human needs
and adorn your throne when you misuse power

I'm here
fulfilling a divine role
and giving birth to the next generation of matriarchs
you intended to incinerate

I started the process of writing this book by running. And because everything moves in cycles, I'm finishing it by running.

Running is painful for my knees, but at the same time, it's medicine for my soul. I can't explain it, and I make peace with the fact that I never will. Sure, science will inform me about the processes that occur in my body and brain when I run that contribute to why I feel this way—but it is more than that. Every time I run, I have a group of incredible women who come into my sentipensante.

Running became my medicine as I started the process of writing this book because many of the beloved women in my life found their wings and left this earthly plane. My grief was so much bigger than my desire to keep moving. But when I was ready, I faced the jaguar, as well as the absence of these women who had inspired me so much. I faced my resentment and anger at the sickness that took them from their children and their lives. It was then that I realized that they are still with me.

My running is spiritual, for with every step, I embody each of these women in my life who faced struggles but who also triumphed through all that they overcame. In some ways, I run *for* them—but, more accurately, I run *with* them.

When I run, I run with all my *amigas-hermanas* (sister-friends) who are gone from this plane, as well as those who are still alive. I am running for those who are going through chemotherapy. I am running with the women putting their bodies through extended and expensive treatments to become mothers, and those who accept that their bodies cannot bear children. I am running with those whose lives have given them the incredible assignment of raising their children alone, and those who take on the mother role, navigating complex family dynamics, sometimes feeling like outsiders due to the lack of a biological connection. I'm running with those struggling to meet their needs, as well as those who are scared because they don't know if leaving their partners will be the best choice. I'm running with those who are waiting to hear from their loved ones in jail or their loved ones who've been deployed in the military, as well as those who cry for leaving family and friends behind as they escape to find a better life. I'm running with those who feel like strangers in their own workplace or the places where they have been re-planted, and with those who've built a new life from the ground up and still believe they don't deserve to be here. I'm running with those whose hearts were broken and who broke the hearts of others. I'm running with the ones drowning in regrets and self-doubt, believing they don't have the grace to receive forgiveness for their aborted fetuses, their aborted dreams of happiness with a partner, their aborted dreams of being who they are. I'm running with those who are preparing for their death and are not yet ready to leave this life. I'm running for the young ones who are in their own race as they attempt to leave their mark. I am running with those whose sentipensante is filled with sensation and those whose sentipensante is filled with numbness.

And I am running with you, beloved friend. I see you. I feel you. I sense your presence. Let my legs feel your frustration and your hurt, as well as your courage and your joy. Yes, I am tired and in pain, my breathing is compromised, and my body feels ready to give up . . . but I won't. So, please don't give up, either. Know that you are wrapped inside my manta. Breathe deeply and let yourself feel that.

During my runs, when I embody the jaguar, my legs feel weak and powerful all at once. I also see the elder comadres, including my abuelitas, watching and cheering me from afar. They sacrificed their dreams and all the things they wanted in order to be the mothers their children needed; now, from a distance, they are so grateful that I and future generations of matriarchs are fulfilling our calling in the world. We, who have worked to reconcile our wounds and offer our medicine, are so very supported.

I take off my manta for them, for my amigas-hermanas, for you. I lay it down on the ground, and together, we weave it back into the Earth. The Earth, embodying an elder herself, fixes my braids, kisses my forehead, blesses me, blows on me three times, and with a voice that is both strong and soft, says, "Thank you for running toward me. Now that we meet, I can see my children in you. Go—keep running and know I'm behind you."

In this way, I am inspired to keep going, even when I want to stop. I'm sure you've felt similarly in your own life. You've lived through your own challenges, and there were times when you wanted to give up, but something inspired you to keep going, to persevere. I know, because you picked up this book. You recognized that, on some level, you had a calling. You were responsible for something larger than just yourself.

Running became a way for me to answer the jaguar's call and to be more proximate to all those whom I long to care for and to wrap in my manta—including the dead and the living. In fact, embodiment practices (including dancing, singing, and other forms of physical activity that engage your full sentipensante) can be very powerful. They allow the multidimensions of time and space to dissolve. They let you see past the veils to all your beloved ancestors and the spirits who watch over you, encouraging you to keep going. They help you to see the brave generations of women—abuelas, madres, amigas-hermanas—who are with you, just as you are with them.

During my embodiment as the jaguar, I kept asking myself: What's next? I saw it clearly: Through this book, I'm here to make the invisible visible and easily sensed. I am here to support you, beloved friend, in creating your own narrative and weaving your own manta—and ultimately, becoming the future matriarch who weaves the manta for the next generations.

I leave you with one final way to ritualize your movement through reconciling with your roots, healing through ancestral wisdom, and reclaiming your own autonomy, beloved friend.

MIRROR AND EMBODY THE JAGUAR
Sacred Contracts for Life

- In what ways do you choose to embody the jaguar? This may be through physical embodiment, such as running, or a deeper connection to Nature and the elements. Prioritize this in your life. Feel the primal strength of the jaguar under your own skin.

- What is your manta? Is it the medicine and poetry of your words? Is it the support you offer through your strength and presence? Is it the altars you build to your ancestors? Is it the indoor and outdoor sanctuaries you create? There is no one way to create your manta—the only requirement is that it comes from your full sentipensante. How are you weaving your manta and self-breeding yourself as a matriarch?

- We, the matriarchs, are meant to tend the fire instead of expanding it. It is our role to keep those in our village sheltered, and to offer order and warmth. We are here to weave our wisdom, and also share it with the young, so they can continue weaving the manta—and so they can remember they are never alone. How can you nurture their process? Consider ways of using all the tools in this book, including the KARE method, to support yourself and others.

- As you create your sacred contracts to continue embodying the jaguar, as well as weaving your manta and wrapping it around your village, be sure to call in Nature—who is lovingly safeguarding parts of your nuna. Please also call in the women in your life, imagining that the threads you spin are connecting to them and providing succor and warmth. Bring in your mothers, grandmothers, sisters, daughters, nieces, and granddaughters. Bring in those who are here and in the unseen realm. Remember that what impacts you impacts each and every one of them.

This is your sacred contract, and it is ongoing and meant to keep you protected and sheltered, even as you protect and shelter others.

As you continue the powerful work of reconciliation, within and without, please know that every word woven throughout this book is intentional, placed with an awareness of your presence. Even if we have never met, we belong to each other. And how do I know we belong to each other? Because I have been weaving you into my braids since the times before my time. I carry you in my sentipensate. Each of my chosen words carries ancestral wisdom and its own energetic charge and exchange. I wanted to honor that, and honor you, by choosing words that are not mere regurgitations of concepts you've already encountered. Rather, they are meant to evoke and stir that which lives not only in your mind, but also in your heart.

My intention throughout this book is to offer you the opportunity to taste your own strength and freedom, and to feel your courage deep in your bones. My wish is that you use your autonomy to co-create the narrative that belongs to your current, unique circumstances—not to be interpreted through my or anyone else's lens! After all, this book was written to awaken the matriarchs on the horizon, those who will nurture others by holding vital roles that embody wisdom, strength, and stability to everyone in their villages. Thus, beloved friend, amiga, comadre, you join an illustrious global lineage. You, too, can be a keeper of history and culture, and support those who grieve because they are wandering through the wilderness without tender assurance and the awareness of grace.

And now, you are also a part of my manta and the larger manta of existence. None of us are isolated threads; we all belong to one another's villages. You were not meant to be alone, and you will never be alone. Your seed grows deep roots, so you will break the soil to find the sun.

Waters will come, winds will pass, and your grace will shine in the eternal colors of the flower you are. The hummingbirds and bees will feed on your medicine, and the jaguar who watches from the distance will rejoice in seeing you flourish.

Until we see each other again, may your winds take you to exactly where you need to be.

Lorena

ACKNOWLEDGMENTS

I question whether to start my list of acknowledgments with those who are here in the living world or list the ones whom I can't see anymore but can feel.

Editorial protocol will suggest one thing, culture and spiritual tradition will say something different, and my sentipensante is leading me to start with the ones in the unseen world because, after all, they may not be in the physical, but I want to believe that they are choosing—in a way—to be near me as much as I want them to be near me to celebrate.

So, my list starts with the Divine force and the God of my understanding who allowed me to be here at this precise moment in history. This force has many forms and shapes and addresses, sometimes is a nourishing force and other times, a protective figure.

Next is Nature, which, with all its complexities, continues to teach me so much about how to be human.

My abuelitas and greatest teachers and inspiration, Rosa Graciela and Ana Isabel, have been by my side every single day during the process of writing this book and even before I knew I wanted to write it. When I felt lost because of the overwhelming responsibilities of this incredible opportunity, I called for their protection and wisdom, and they showed up one way or another. On days when I didn't know where to begin, they had a way of making themselves known by reminding me that this book was not just a book. It is medicine to awaken other granddaughters. Every day, I lit a candle and burned palo santo, asking them to give me strength and wisdom to use the exact words you, my beloved friend, needed to hear. I feel their manta holding me and carrying me. I feel their voice and presence. Gracias, abuelitas.

Mamá Tulia, your recent passing left a hole in my manta because, after my grandmothers, you were the embodiment and the finest representation of what a matriarch is supposed to be. Thank you for taking me in and loving me as your own when I re-planted myself in the US. You were a master of transforming friendships into family and how to live spiritually, with freedom and no restrictions.

Mamá Doris, you inspire courage, reinvention, and love for learning and reading. I wish life would give me enough time to read all the incredible books I've inherited from you. The pieces of your story shared by my husband—your son—were fuel when I doubted the writing process. I feel your tenacious spirit on every page of this book.

Madrina Rocio, you taught me what it means to be a trustworthy confidant, and you embodied the meaning of a genuine secret holder. Always quiet and observant, and an innate teacher of conscious listening, ready to listen to others. Your docile and vivid spirit is missed profoundly, but I feel you closer to my heart every time I light a candle and the smoke of tobacco dances in the wind as I listen to Peruvian music.

Becky, my throat still feels the aftertaste of your passing during the last stretch of writing this book. I don't live moved by regrets, but I sincerely wish you could have seen the end of the book. You completely redefined what it is to be resilient and protective of the self, and why it is important to celebrate life. You were such a virtuosa of living within sacred boundaries, and I learned so much in the last few months of your three-and-a-half years of battling metastasized cancer. You taught me to respect my space, and that saying no was an act of self-care. I know that you are with me, like you said, always and forever. Gracias, amiga.

I come from a very long line of enduring ancestors. When I feel alone and full of fear of where the path as a writer will take me, I close my eyes, and I can feel them all around me, holding my hand and opening paths.

Okay, now to the living:

My beloved mejor amigo, best friend, and cheerleader, Mark. Pages of a book will not be enough to thank you for all you have done for me, not only for your support with the book but for believing in me and for telling me how proud you are of me. Your loving and reassuring words and your constant generous and loving acts were (and still are) powerful medicine for me that mended my broken trust in men. I love you!

My mom, Marianella, is a symbol of spiritual strength and nourishment. Her enthusiastic tone and pride in her voice every time I accomplish something is contagious. My mom is a woman of faith and a pillar of surrender to God's goodness, with the drive of a jaguar. My dad, Roberto, taught me to ask questions and not to believe until I have proof, a genuine example of an inquisitive mind. I feel so grateful for the parents that life chose for me.

I'm so blessed to have a healthy relationship with my siblings. Despite our different points of view, we know that we belong to each other, and no matter what, we will support each other. My sister, Fátima, is my best friend in the world and my truest refuge when I look for uncomplicated love. She has been there with her big ears and heart to hear about all my challenges and celebrate my victories. My brothers, Cristiam and Gustavo, are so different from each other, yet they are the strong shoulders I need when the floor is shaking. I love my siblings because they love and accept me as I am.

Being a stepmom has been a blessing for my womanhood, and this amazing journey of taking into my life the lives of two younger boys has had its ups and downs. Jarek and Nathanael are my central motivation to be a good human, a good woman, and a good mother figure. They have taught me the true essence of acceptance and tolerance. I learned to love unconditionally, to let go, and to trust that they receive all they need to become the amazing adults they are. My sentipensante loves them beyond words.

For my teachers and mentors:

It is said that a wise teacher is like a hidden treasure, imparting knowledge and inspiring you to seek your own truth and enriching your soul with their wisdom. I have been blessed with incredible teachers along my path. I can't think of a better tribute to their generosity than to publicly thank them for their wisdom and constant support.

Tara, your work has impacted my healing journey from the very beginning. Life moved us closer, and you became a friend—my comadre—and a reliable point of reference on each step of my path. Your trust in my gold served me as a compass and refuge. One day, when I was deep in self-doubt, you asked me, "What do you think I see in you?" My response was, "A diamond that needs to be polished." You paused and answered, "No, my dear, you are a diamond already shining." These words changed the trajectory of my life. Thank you!

Daniel, you opened your heart and your house to me, and it was through your caring that I was able to awaken and recuperate the wisdom of my grandmothers buried under lots of emotional pain. Your ways of guiding me through mysticism and cultural sovereignty were instrumental in guiding me to embody my spiritual self. Our days-long pilgrimages, talking and reintroducing myself to Nature, will forever be remembered with gratitude.

Ayya Dhammadīpā, when I needed a teacher who could understand the complexity of the Latino culture and its intersection with multiple spiritualities, you were there and are still there for me. Your exquisite advice to keep asking and inquiring about how to live my spirituality without the restrictions of dogmatic barriers is a refuge to me. How you have navigated multiple worlds and cultures is an inspiration and serves as a corrective course to recalibrate my aspirations and vision of this book. I am grateful for you.

Jonathan, your refined way of delivering abstract and etheric concepts in a pragmatic, embodied, and current manner keeps me inspired. You made ancient philosophies so relevant to me. I am so grateful for your trust and for openly offering me the freedom to explore my curious mind.

Felicia, Lisa, and Luisa, without your supportive nature, your time, and your willingness to accompany me through the years of self-inquiry and reconciliation, this book would still be a project. Thank you for the countless hours of undivided attention, conscious listening, and emotional homework.

Okay, now, about those who supported me in working on this book:

Nirmala Nataraj, from the very beginning, I asked the mountains to bring me the right person who could polish my words. When we met, I knew that you would understand the heart behind my writing. Your gift of seeing all the layers of a rough idea and the way you guide me to contextualize my ideas with elegance is simply remarkable. Thank you for the long hours of digging through years of material and pulling the jewels needed to build the manuscript.

Amanda Orozco, we crossed paths at an unusual intersection. When I was in desperate need of an agent who could guide me through the ups and downs of publishing a book for the first time, you came through. Thank you for trusting my work and for safeguarding my back and path.

Devon Halliday, when I was toward the end of my writing process, seeking a broader perspective, your fresh eyes and assessment supported me to refine my story and stay true to what matters most. Thank you for your clarity in making this book a true reflection of who I am.

Jaime Schwalb and Angela Wix at Sounds True, I deeply appreciate your guidance through the process of writing and publishing this book and for seeing the value of my words.

Reid Tracy and Kelly Notaras, with your Authorpreneur program and writers' workshops, I found the top-tier programs that helped me shape my vision of what I wanted this book to be.

Thank you to the Coalition of Hispanic Artists (CHA) for seeing my poetry as innovative and needed in our Hispanic community in the US, and for your commitment to highlighting the talents of artists living in the US who would otherwise be unknown.

Now, for my friends and colleagues:

I learned that there are many types of friendships in life and that I have my own way of loving and relating to my friends. Seasonal friends have been so profoundly important to my emotional sovereignty. Like sandpaper rubbing the edges of uneven and rough surfaces, these people had to be there so I could become who I am—and to them, I am deeply grateful.

Thank you, friends from school, college, and advanced-studies programs. A heartfelt thank you to the Academia Mayor de la Lengua Quechua and *Yachachiq* (teacher) Julia Qquenaya Apaza and her Quechua editing of the book. Thank you, friends from the Latino community at my local church. My sincere gratitude to my friends from the Washington, DC area, especially to OHM and family; your support will be eternally engraved in my heart. My time in Tampa, Florida was pivotal, and many thanks to my friends from Hispanic Professional Women's Association (HPWA), especially Margarita Gonzalez, Pilar Ortiz, Nelcy Baltz, Imelda Dutton, Catalina Botero, and Ana Vargas. How could I forget my networking buddy, Tony Selvaggio?

For years, I owned and operated Hanaq Prana Wellness Center and had thousands of clients and students. This section of this book would be incomplete if I didn't give my gratitude to each of those humans who do embodiment practices like yoga, mindful movement, therapeutic dance, and sound; as well as those who sat in meditation, trained, and traveled to retreats with me. Special thanks to Debbie Palombo, Vinita Witanachchi, and Edith Velez, my three loyal first members. I had the honor of having these incredible teachers on staff, and I give so many thanks to LeGrand Jones, Nicole R. Grannie, and Amanda Laseter.

Being in the health and wellness industry for decades has given me the chance to connect with many people and colleagues, and to all of you, thank you. And special gratitude goes, in no particular order, to those who checked in on me during the writing process and kept me motivated to finish. Thank you: Jennifer Womer Kreatsoulas, Babette Dunkelgrün, Mariana Restrepo, Pamela Stokes-Eggleston, Kristina Graf, Christy Sharshel, Cindy Novelo, and Michael Cohen.

To be part of spiritual communities has been crucial to me. I'm grateful for my friends and their support: IMCW and Spanish Café con Leche and Wednesday night sanghas, Dassanāya Buddhist Community, and my spiritual comadres from my peer group with MMTCP, Camila Rodriguez, Andrea Alvarez, Maria Restrepo, J. Vecchia.

My profound appreciation to these humans who heard about this book and encouraged me to continue writing it: Alejandra Mendoza,

Daniel Quispe, Nataly Mendocilla, Rosario Yacota, Karina Alvarez, Sandra Medina, Milagros Alessi, Rocio Reynoso, Marita Cisneros and family, Carol Zamora, Daniela Succar, Yandy Huaranga, Juan Francisco Apaza, Don Francisco Apaza Flores, Francisco Victoria, Don Aurelio Ortiz Huaricallo, Clara Sanchez, Heather Filipowicz, Grace de Ruales, Miluska Paredes, Cecilia Dexter, Dominique Ferrera Hawkins, Pepe Ramos, Genevieve Wall, Sergio Merino, and all of those who I keep in my sentipensante.

Like many out there, I've also had my fair share of rejection and disregard in the professional field. In honor of those who have ever felt ignored and who haven't had their contributions taken seriously, I'm taking a moment to acknowledge all those whose paths I crossed who didn't acknowledge my existence, didn't believe in me, and who dismissed me. In their eyes, I wasn't qualified, I didn't have enough education or influence, or I was simply a rebel swimming against the stream and disrupting normality. In truth, I wasn't disobeying the norm; I was embodying the jaguar and weaving the lost, almost forgotten threads of a broken manta. I know who you are, and you know who you are. Thank you for being the logs that my fire needed.

ABOUT THE AUTHOR

Lorena Saavedra Smith is a Pacha philosopher and ecopsychologist. Originally from Perú and re-planted to the US, Lorena is a lifelong storyteller and keeper of Andean ancestral wisdom and medicine.

With more than two decades of experience in the wellness industry, Lorena draws on a multidisciplinary background to support others in finding healing through inner wisdom and the power of Nature.

Lorena's personal story includes migrating to the US in her early twenties, facing and overcoming abusive interpersonal relationships, and navigating the transformative journey of re-planting into her new environment. Her personal wounds have become the portals through which she has reconnected to, reconciled with, and remembered her medicine, which offers readers the key to personal and collective healing through a weaving of ancestral medicine and future possibilities.

Anchored to the principle of reciprocity with Nature, Lorena's work and legacy are centered on educating people through thought-provoking presentations on emotional and spiritual autonomy. She inspires audiences to harness the power of their cultural heritage as a means of addressing stress and mental-health challenges, and to reconnect with Nature as an essential aspect of their overall well-being.

Through her words and work, she hopes to support readers from a variety of backgrounds—especially re-planted Latinas—to move through anxiety, shame, and perfectionism; to rediscover and reconnect with their own inner wisdom; and to access the tools for interweaving their dreams with their deep roots, enabling them to navigate the struggles of the modern human and planetary challenges and emerge triumphant.

She's a proud spouse of a US Navy veteran and splits her time between Perú and the Washington, DC metro area.

You can connect with Lorena through her website, lorenasaavedrasmith.com.

ABOUT SOUNDS TRUE

Sounds True was founded in 1985 by Tami Simon with a clear mission: to disseminate spiritual wisdom. Since starting out as a project with one woman and her tape recorder, we have grown into a multimedia publishing company with a catalog of more than 3,000 titles by some of the leading teachers and visionaries of our time, and an ever-expanding family of beloved customers from across the world.

In more than three decades of evolution, Sounds True has maintained our focus on our overriding purpose and mission: to wake up the world. We offer books, audio programs, online learning experiences, and in-person events to support your personal growth and awakening, and to unlock our greatest human capacities to love and serve.

At SoundsTrue.com you'll find a wealth of resources to enrich your journey, including our weekly *Insights at the Edge* podcast, free downloads, and information about our nonprofit Sounds True Foundation, where we strive to remove financial barriers to the materials we publish through scholarships and donations worldwide.

To learn more, please visit SoundsTrue.com/freegifts or call us toll-free at 800.333.9185.

Together, we can wake up the world.